White Water Handbook

2nd Edition

by John T. Urban

Revised by
T. Walley Williams III

**Appalachian
Mountain Club**

ISBN 0-910146-28-4

PREFACE
TO FIRST EDITION

From the time when the ice first goes out in March until the last snow leaves the high northern slopes at the end of May, the rivers of the Northeast offer rewarding sport for the skilled paddler. The pleasures of white water are old, but much is new — boats and techniques have been changing radically, and these developments have given the paddler an enhanced command over his craft in the rapids and made of slalom competitions lively contests of paddling virtuosity. Lore has given way to technique — a technique which can be as specific as one's ability to assess the patterns of the river, and which can be, at least to a considerable extent, compressed between covers.

Many of us learned what we know of white water piecemeal. We talked among ourselves and read what was to be found. We tried new boats and new techniques. We had some glorious runs and were occasionally washed down a rapid when our boats declined our guidance and our company. We continued to discover our ignorance when meeting new problems, when running new rivers, when teaching friends who were new to white water, and when learning from those who were old to it. In all this we sharpened our skill, always narrowing the gap between the actual and the possible.

This handbook is intended to make learning on the river easier through preparation. It can supplement, but never substitute for, thorough instruction and growing experience. It is a verbal summary of what must come to be in the paddler's mind and muscle, a systematic background for the experience to be had from instruction and his own experimenting.

In writing this handbook I have been the beneficiary, known and unknown, of many people. Among those who have helped with suggestions and comments are Robert Bliss,

G. Sargent Janes, Paul McElroy, Gardner Moulton, John W. Nevins, Jr., Lisl Urban, and Thomas Wilson. Like many others, I am grateful to Barbara Wright for her contagious enthusiasm for the kayak and its technique, and to many friends in the Appalachian Mountain Club for a cheerful companionship on a multitude of rivers, in technical discussion, and in a number of practical experiments on critical stability. Francelia Mason has greatly enhanced the text with most of the illustrations. Photographs are by the author. The Appalachian Mountain Club has provided an immensely congenial climate for white water paddling and for writing this handbook.

John T. Urban
Cambridge, Massachusetts
June, 1965

PREFACE
TO SECOND EDITION

When a fast-changing sport such as white water boating leads to a book, it is inevitable that obsolescence will set in quickly. New techniques and new equipment eventually lead to a need for revising manuscripts or starting over.

The trouble with revision is that it usually involves major surgery. If the editor is not the original author, the work is either a new work or the original is left in a shambles.

This second edition was purposely done in a way that preserves as much of the original as possible. Three new chapters on paddle strokes and technique have been added, while only minor changes have been made elsewhere. The new technique chapters are those on tandem and solo canoe paddling by myself, and the chapter on kayak paddling by Leslie Eden.

The chapters that describe how a boater interacts with the river have been altered as little as possible. Of course, the result is some duplication of information in the old and new sections. This is not a bad situation. One often needs to have information about a sport presented from several points of view before it makes sense.

Safety is another area where the sport has continued to grow. Numerous articles in the *American Whitewater Journal* have introduced us to new ideas and techniques, and many ideas have come from boaters in the Appalachian Mountain Club. These have been gathered together in two new chapters. The first, "Coping with River Hazards Safely," combines the information from the first edition with much new material. The second, "Organizing for Safety and Enjoyment," is an attempt to pass on the trip-leading lore of the Appalachian Mountain Club for use by other groups. It may seem at first that techniques for leading 48-boat trips would have little relevance to three friends off for a day trip, but the need for safety is the same. One need only ignore material specific to large groups.

Equipment is a third area where there has been vast change in fifteen years, so a new chapter has been prepared to update people on what is available and how to keep it in repair. Here, particular thanks are in order to Charlie Walbridge, who has introduced us to the throw bag for keeping a rescue line organized and ready up to the moment it is needed, and to the Nantahala Outdoor Center, whose teaching program has greatly influenced boaters all over the eastern United States and whose catalog photographs have been used to illustrate the chapter on equipment.

No preface would be complete without a section thanking the other contributors to a book. While a few names come to mind because of their recent influence, the reader should understand that this book is really the work of an active canoe-ing program of an active club. For instance, the checklist for leaders in the chapter on organization is the result of a day-long meeting in 1979 of the AMC Interchapter Canoe Com-mittee. Many of the diagrams are based on the drawings of Don D'Entremont, prepared for the Boston Chapter's begin-ner instruction program when Roger Marshall was instruction chairman. The solo instruction program of Marlene Schroeder produced much new material for the solo techniques chapter. New techniques were also introduced from the southern Ap-palachians by Dave and Posie Dauphine, Tom Doyle, and Jan Costa. Finally, there are two boaters who had great personal influence on this editor — Louise Davis, who got me hooked on canoeing in the early sixties, and Biff Manhard, who had the greatest influence in getting me into canoe instruction.

I would also like to thank my wife, Lynn Williams, for taking the photos in the canoeing technique chapters. Dave and Leslie Eden took the kayaking photos, and Dave Eden con-tributed some of the kayaking drawings. Betsey Tryon of the

AMC staff provided the other drawings in the new chapters. Drawings and photos in the river running chapters were provided by John Urban. Production work at the AMC was done by Robert Saunders and Michael Cirone. Arlyn Powell provided editorial assistance. Salina Press printed the book.

T. Walley Williams III
Belmont, Massachusetts
February, 1981

CONTENTS

I

Introduction

What is white water? It is a light boat in a fast rapid, a game of skill played against a river, a sport in which wit and subtlety outrank muscle. It is the passage of a wilderness stream, a weekend's paddling for its own sake, and the few intense minutes of effort and precision of a slalom race. The constant elements are skill in handling the boat and a close knowledge of the ways of moving water.

The modern canoe comes in a direct line from the North American Indians, who used their boats much as we do, if more earnestly. Like ours, their canoes were designed to carry wilderness duffel, to survive rough stretches of open water, or to run difficult rapids, and the various shapes they evolved were remarkably like those we use today. The most striking difference is quite recent — the specialized white water canoe now has a completely enclosed hull, like a kayak, and since it is intended for sport alone it may be small in all dimensions and provide for no more than minimum duffel. Modern technique in running rapids is, in a sense, matched to these boats; the shoe-keeled open canoe of appropriate design and dimension

1

can be used with enjoyment, but the standard fin-keeled lake canoe is not at home in this water, although it can be used with some success, if less pleasure, in the more moderate rapids.

The kayak comes to us from the Eskimos by way of Europe, where it was adapted from the original slim hunting craft, first for comfortable river touring, and more recently for rapids paddling. The touring kayak, single or double, like the lake canoe, is awkward in rapids, where agility and responsiveness are primary requirements, but the evolution of design of the single kayak within the last two decades has made of it a superb white water boat. Completely watertight, light and responsive, it can negotiate involved passages and heavy waves with sure ease in expert hands. Small and efficient, it makes the best use of the paddler's effort and makes good time on the river; low in the water, it is relatively unaffected by wind. It demands a polished technique, however, for it is designed to have little inherent stability, and the paddler must depend upon his paddle to stay upright in turbulent water and strong currents. He must also be able to roll back up after a capsize. It has the specific disadvantages of limited duffel capacity, a lower and therefore poorer view of the river ahead, and relative uselessness in rescue work.

Until a fairly short time ago, the shoe-keeled canoe was the preferred rapids boat, for it was nimbler than the touring kayak, whose technique was limited to strokes to move forward and backward, to steer, and to stabilize with a low brace in the rear quarter. Moderate beam combined with the low center of gravity make the kayak stable, but at the expense of maneuverability. In 1953 Milo Duffek, a Czech paddler, showed that the canoeist's draw stroke could be adapted in a revolutionary way to the narrow-beamed kayak. He reached far out from the boat, paddle held high, to use his blade as a combined pivot point and support for his weight. This stroke, requiring a strong lean to the side, made the very instability of the narrow kayak a prime virtue, for it allowed the paddler not only to turn abruptly, but to oppose the capsizing effects of powerful crosscurrents by leaning sharply against them.

Introduction

The canoeist in his turn saw that leaning against a current or a turn did not belong exclusively to the kayak, but could be equally effective as part of his own technique. He, too, learned to commit his weight to the paddle against the inertia of a strong countercurrent and to use the paddle as a far pivot point to the inside of a turn.

Not so many years ago the backflow of an eddy was thought to be a sure trap for the unwary paddler — let him poke his bow into it and he was lost, a sure dunker through the malevolent grip of the countercurrents at the eddy line. Rather let him set into it, stern first, and he was safe and at rest. This is now ancient history; we paddle forward into eddies as a matter of course, and the dynamic style of paddling is no more daring than riding a bicycle. But it is more fun, and safer just because it extends the paddler's control of his boat.

The lone paddler is a figure of romantic splendor in the imagination. Completely self-reliant, he travels swiftly and confidently on the wilderness stream. For white water, this is nonsense. Any paddler had better have some able companions on that stream, for he will need them urgently a few times in his life, and will be grateful often enough for their presence and help. The novice who has expert friends is fortunate; if he does not, he should join a club. There he can develop his skill, find companionship through mutual interest, and learn the extent to which safety in the rapids is a matter of mutual responsibility.

Each season brings its fresh stories of rash canoeists who, cheerfully unaware of the fundamentals of white water, have taken canoes into rapids to risk, and lose, their lives. In every fatal accident one inevitably finds at least two of the following — inexperience, very cold water, failure to use a life preserver, or absence of a support party. And, swimming in the rapids is no easier if one has a canoeing manual in one's pocket. Errors of judgment and acts of ignorance can be costly or fatal.

To run a lively rapid you must be neat, quick, and decisive — therein is the pleasure. The penalty is a ducking, and

3

perhaps a damaged boat. If the expert does not always go free, he will run the ordinary rapids with impunity and have a reasonable expectation for the really difficult ones as well. It may take daring to get into a rough drop, but only a cool appraisal of its demands and a matching skill in meeting them will get you through it. For this you need much practice based on competent instruction.

White water technique is not self-evident — it only seems so in retrospect — and this handbook is planned to give the elements of this technique, together with some understanding of the water on which it is practiced, of boats and equipment, and of the elements of safety. In a sport like this one, reading about technique is no substitute for practice, but it can make that practice much more worthwhile. It can also call attention to a multitude of details for which experience need not be the teacher.

For example, a novice canoeist tied his painters neatly into the thwarts; half an hour later this made the rescue of his swamped canoe doubly difficult. A canoeist wore a poncho on a rainy day, capsized, and found himself sluiced an extra hundred rocky yards downriver trying to get unwrapped. Details can be crucial. So can standard aspects of technique. One canoeist, starting an upstream ferry out of an eddy, entered the current at too great an angle and was carried broadside downstream for some distance. He barely avoided being swept into a bouldery falls just below. Had he practiced this maneuver where there was no penalty, the technique would have been at hand when needed.

The experienced boater too easily assumes that his own understanding is shared by all; the beginner is often not aware of the narrow limits of his experience. Instruction bridges this gap, and if it begins in a quasi-formal fashion, it continues as long as people paddle together.

In instruction there are mutual obligations. The beginner should expect skilled teaching and example. But first he must be qualified — he must be in good physical condition, for this is a strenuous and sometimes taxing sport; he must be able to swim well; and he should be able to handle his boat well in smooth water, for it is neither practical nor safe to learn basic canoeing or kayaking in fast water. And, in addition to learning the use of the boat itself, he should be so familiar with the principles of safety in white water that his reactions to threatened or actual trouble will be nearly automatic, so that he will avoid or minimize it for himself and effectively help others.

II

Strokes and Techniques for Paddling a Canoe Tandem

GETTING READY TO STUDY STROKES

Most of the important work in canoeing involves an interaction of the canoeist's paddle with the water. For learning purposes it is convenient to organize these interactions into strokes; however, the beginner should keep in mind that the experienced boater uses his paddle in many ways and that not all of them will have names. After mastering the standard strokes, variations and "in between" strokes will come to mind naturally as the boater continues the process of mastering his environment.

It is important to say from the start that not all strokes involve motion of the blade with respect to the paddler. Often the paddle is used as a rudder to change the direction of a moving boat. In general, if one can use a rudder stroke, it is less work than an active stroke and thus more desirable; however, for teaching purposes the formal strokes that require the paddler to move his blade will be discussed first. Following the active strokes a separate section on rudder strokes will make this important use of the paddle clear.

7

Two Ways to Think about Strokes. There are two ways to think about strokes, and both are necessary for mastering white water boating. The first is to consider the path the paddle blade makes as it passes through the water. In the following sections this path is emphasized by showing overhead bird's eye views of the paddler and the path made by the paddle during each stroke.

The second way to think about a stroke is to consider how the body and limbs must be placed and how they must move. Here both diagrams and photos will be helpful.

How to Place the Hands on the Paddle. Study the photos in this section. In every one the paddler has the grip hand placed squarely over the end of the tee grip on the paddle while the other hand is wrapped around the shaft. All fingers of this hand are around the paddle so that the forearm applies a force perpendicular to the shaft.

Where to Place the Hands on the Paddle. The crisp, precise strokes of the white water expert require a different hand placement than that used for paddling hour after hour on flat water. Both paddlers place the upper hand on the end of the shaft in the same way; however, the flat water paddler prefers to have his lower hand as far down the shaft as is comfortable, while in white water the hands are as close together as is comfortable. Closer hands require more strength to move the paddle in the water, but they allow for much more speed in the recovery part of a stroke and they permit the paddle to be placed in the water farther from the boat. In addition, several strokes, such as the cross high brace and cross back stroke, cannot be done at all with the hands far apart.

Using Strong Body Muscles. Good boating depends on using the strong trunk and back muscles rather than the weaker arm muscles. Pay particular attention to the elbows. They may flex or extend during the recovery part of the stroke, but during the power phase they remain relatively fixed while the body bends or twists. In the photos that illustrate the individual strokes, the position of the arms and body is shown at the beginning of the power phase.

Kneeling in White Water. All white water strokes will be described for a paddler who is kneeling, with the buttocks resting against a seat or thwart. For long stretches of easy paddling sitting on the seats is all right, but kneeling is safer and more powerful in most circumstances.

The Naming of Strokes. The name of a stroke is often a description of the path taken by the paddle blade in the water. The name is modified by the word "back" if it reverses the usual direction and by the word "cross" if the paddle crosses over to the opposite side of the boat with no shift in hand grip. However, there are other ways to name the strokes, so it is well to "translate" the meaning of each name as it is met.

Practicing Paddle Strokes in Calm Water. Even Olympic paddlers use calm water for perfecting paddling technique. Use white water only for learning techniques that require current. Paddle strokes can be learned in calm water. Rudder and maneuvering strokes merely require one to paddle ahead fast before trying to turn.

THE FORWARD STROKE AND ITS VARIATIONS

The forward stroke begins with the *reach*. The shaft arm is fully extended at the elbow and the same shoulder is rotated as far forward as possible. The upper grip arm is placed in front of the paddler with the hand over the water. Adjust the upper arm to place the paddle in the water as far forward as possible. A good paddler uses a little of the forward momentum of the paddle during the recovery phase of the previous stroke to fully extend his arm, shoulder, and body muscles so that the blade enters the water a few extra inches farther forward during the catch phase.

In the *catch* phase the blade suddenly enters the water and starts backward, powered by a forward motion of the upper torso.

Figure 1. The continuous motion of a powerful forward stroke can be analyzed into six phases.

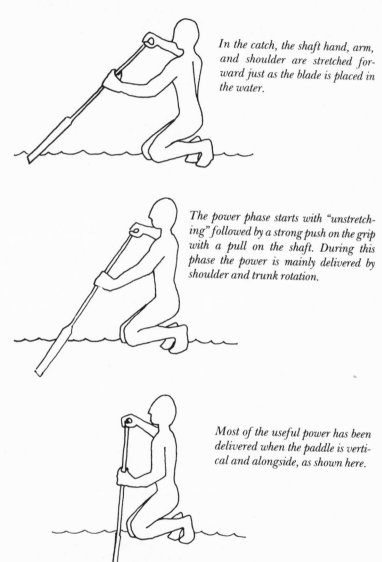

In the catch, the shaft hand, arm, and shoulder are stretched forward just as the blade is placed in the water.

The power phase starts with "unstretching" followed by a strong push on the grip with a pull on the shaft. During this phase the power is mainly delivered by shoulder and trunk rotation.

Most of the useful power has been delivered when the paddle is vertical and alongside, as shown here.

Recover the blade from the water by lowering the grip hand.

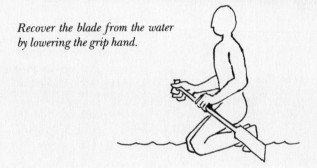

Rotation of the grip hand and cocking of the shaft wrist, feather the blade parallel to the water as it starts forward.

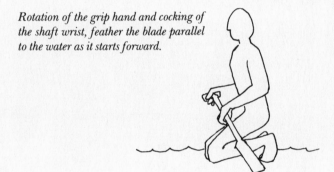

The paddle is about to be rotated back to the first position while the paddler completes the reach.

The *power* phase of the stroke finds the blade moving from far ahead to just alongside the paddler. Most of the power is delivered by rotation of the trunk and the shoulder girdle. There will be very little change in the angle of either arm at the elbows, since arm muscles lack the power for sustained paddling. For an easy recovery, stop applying power when the paddle is alongside and relax as it moves farther back.

The *recovery* is started by dropping the upper hand in toward the center of the boat and twisting the paddle so that the blade is parallel to the water to minimize wind drag as it moves forward. The power face, or face of the blade that pushed on the water during the stroke, is up during the recovery. Near the end of the recovery the hands are still in a horizontal plane; then they quickly rotate until the shaft hand is below and well forward of the grip hand.

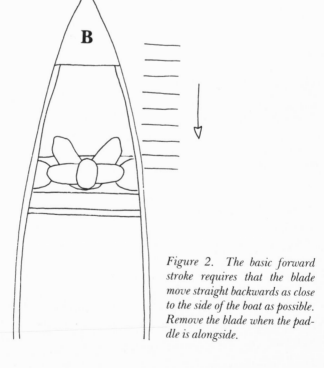

Figure 2. The basic forward stroke requires that the blade move straight backwards as close to the side of the boat as possible. Remove the blade when the paddle is alongside.

Figure 3. Note how the paddler in this front view of the forward stroke tucks the paddle under the boat. The closer the paddle to the keel line, the less it will inadvertently turn the boat.

Adding Power to the Forward Stroke. A tremendous amount of energy is stored in the stretched muscles of the torso during the reach phase of the forward stroke. Most of this energy is released during the catch and first portion of the power phase. Application of power to the paddle past the alongside position merely "lifts water"; it does not move the boat. To increase power, start the recovery when the paddle is alongside. This will result in many short strokes with increased power per stroke.

Champion paddlers work to increase the use of body rotation so that the paddle moves along the side of the boat almost straight up and down rather than changing its angle a lot. With practice this action allows the stroke to come back farther with a vertical blade, which continues to deliver power.

In a good forward stroke the blade is close to the boat. If possible the lower part of the blade should pass under the gunwale.

13

THE FORWARD SWEEP AND C-STROKES

Small corrections in the heading or direction of the boat are best made while paddling rather than by making separate maneuvering strokes. In tandem boating, the bow paddler can push his end of the boat sideways at the very beginning of a forward stroke by altering the path through the water to do the sweep or C-stroke.

The C-stroke is made by placing the paddle a distance away from the centerline during the reach. The catch pulls water toward the center of the boat, then the power phase continues alongside. For a bow paddler on the right, the C-stroke moves the bow to the right.

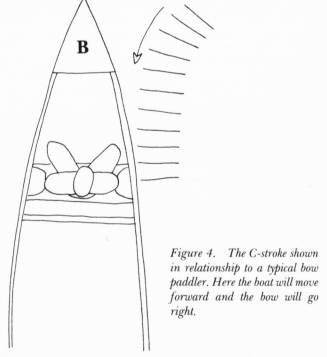

Figure 4. The C-stroke shown in relationship to a typical bow paddler. Here the boat will move forward and the bow will go right.

The sweep stroke has the opposite effect. It starts close to the centerline and sweeps away as shown in figure 5. Figure 6 shows a front view of a paddler doing a sweep. Many paddlers unintentionally do a slight sweep instead of a correct forward stroke. To keep the boat going straight the stern must then do a correction stroke, which wastes energy.

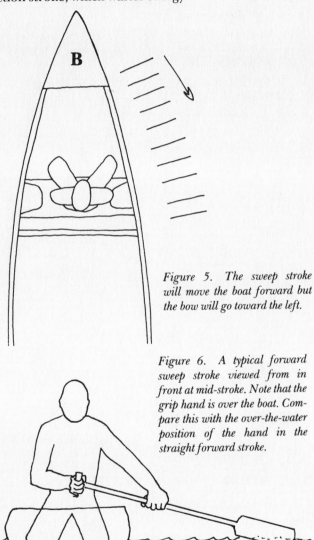

Figure 5. The sweep stroke will move the boat forward but the bow will go toward the left.

Figure 6. A typical forward sweep stroke viewed from in front at mid-stroke. Note that the grip hand is over the boat. Compare this with the over-the-water position of the hand in the straight forward stroke.

When paddling solo, the sweep and C-strokes are invaluable. They are often continued farther back into a full C or sweep.

Stern Forward Sweep. For mild corrections by the stern, the forward sweep stroke looks different, since only the second half of a full sweep will move the boat sideways. Figure 7 shows how the paddle is placed in the water far from the centerline and finishes up close. For a greater degree of correction the sternman will use a draw stroke.

Figure 7.   The path of a forward sweep when used by the sternman for a minor correction.

THE J-STROKE VERSUS THE STERN PRY

For efficiency minor corrections must be made as part of the forward stroke. Only the J-stroke will push the stern as part of a regular forward stroke. For those who find this stroke difficult or tiring, a short reverse sweep or pry stroke described below will have to be used every second or third stroke. The J-stroke is preferred since it allows the rhythm of the paddling to proceed uninterrupted.

The J-stroke takes the same path as the forward stroke, but the blade changes angle part way through as shown in figure 8. To make this change, rotate the grip hand "away" from the body so that the thumb points down toward the water. The resulting change in blade angle will push the blade toward the boat. The paddler must resist this force with the shaft hand by using the relatively weak muscles that abduct the upper arm away from the shoulder. For persons who do not have strength in these muscles, the J-stroke will lead quickly to fatigue.

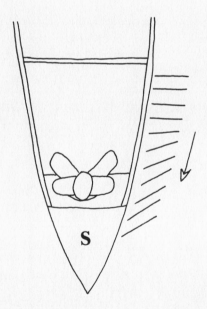

Figure 8.   Path of the J-stroke used by a sternman for a minor correction. Note that the change in blade angle occurs next to the paddler, not far behind. This J-stroke will take the same time as the bow paddler's forward stroke. It is not suitable for use by a solo paddler. (See chapter on "Solo Paddling" for the correct solo J-stroke.)

Reverse Sweep or Stern Pry Correction. As a correction, the stern pry or reverse sweep is done far aft by rotating the grip hand into the thumb up position. It is a short rudder action with the elbow of the shaft hand tucked in against the body to resist the "push." This stroke is less tiring than the J-stroke and has the added advantage that it sets the paddle up for a low brace recovery. It tends to throw the sternman out of rhythm with the bow, though, unless great care is taken. The positions of the hands in the J and reverse sweep strokes can be seen in figures 34 and 36 in the "Solo Paddling" chapter.

THE POWERFUL MANEUVERING STROKES

For the sudden changes in direction required in white water, special turning strokes are required. These strokes will be introduced and discussed as if the boat were still in the water. A separate section will discuss another important use of these strokes — for sudden rudder action when the boat is moving forward.

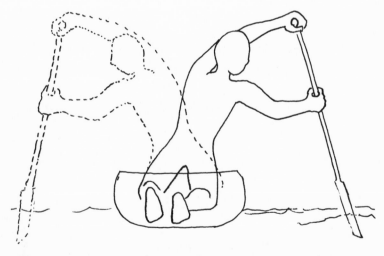

Figure 9.   In the draw stroke the upper arm is in front of the face or forehead and is extended. The lower elbow is partially bent. Motion is imparted to the paddle with the strong trunk muscles.

Draw Stroke. The draw stroke pulls water straight toward the boat from the side. It is a powerful body muscle stroke if properly executed. Study the rear view of the draw in figure 9. Note that the paddle is shown almost vertical. The blade is moved toward the boat by bending the trunk and shoulders. The shaft arm is bent at the elbow at the beginning of the stroke. It is not necessary to appreciably increase this bend. Just hold the arm position and let the trunk muscles do the work.

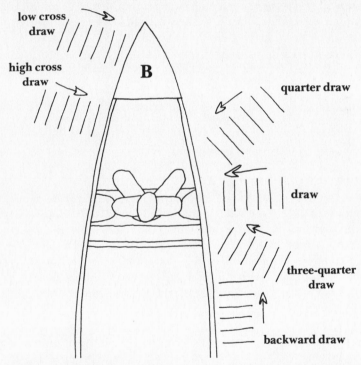

Figure 10. Here all of the draw and cross draw paddle paths are shown for a right-handed paddler.

To learn the draw, arch the upper arm just in front of and higher than your forehead with the hand in front of the opposite shoulder. Hold the end of the paddle and let it hang vertically. Now place the lower hand on the shaft in a comfortable position with the elbow partly flexed. Fix the arms in this position and see how much motion you can achieve by bending the trunk. The paddlers in figure 15 show how a draw stroke should look.

Most of the power in a draw comes from the trunk muscles. Some power comes by pushing with the upper (grip) arm. The muscles of the shaft arm fix the pivot point. They do not actively pull. Study the drawing of the high brace (figure 28). If you pull with the lower arm from a high brace position you will do the typical inefficient "draw" stroke that is seen all too often. It is a poor stroke and should be avoided.

While the draw is usually done so that the blade moves straight toward the centerline of the boat, the body can be rotated to face the draw almost all the way to the stern or almost all the way forward. We will refer to these as a three-quarters draw or a quarter draw stroke. Figure 10 shows how the draw strokes are classified.

Pry Stroke. The true pry stroke is done with the paddle vertical and is most often used by the bow paddler. It uses the boat for a fulcrum. Begin with the paddle shaft parallel to the water and the blade aft and perpendicular to the water. Raise the upper hand so that the blade slices into the water and under the boat at an angle. With both hands, pull toward the centerline of the boat, stopping when the paddle is vertical. When the pry is correctly done, the blade starts out angled under the keel and ends up vertical.

The best recovery is underwater. Rotate the upper hand somewhat and reach forward and out; then repeat the stroke. This takes considerable practice to learn. An alternate recovery is to drop the grip hand forward at the end of the stroke to bring the blade clear of the water. This is preferred at the end of one or two pries when shifting to another stroke. The pry is one of the most powerful white water strokes, especially when used in the bow of a moving boat in deep water. Do not pry in shallow water, since this can cause the paddle to be trapped under the boat, resulting in a spill or a lost paddle. Compare this pry stroke to the stern pry discussed after the cross draw.

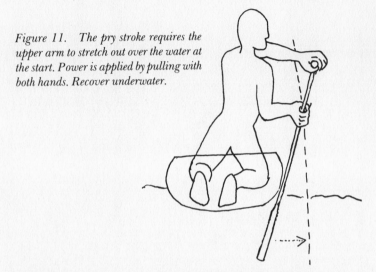

Figure 11.   The pry stroke requires the upper arm to stretch out over the water at the start. Power is applied by pulling with both hands. Recover underwater.

Cross Draw. The cross draw enables a bow paddler to move the boat toward the off-paddle side. To learn this stroke, kneel with your paddle in the normal paddling position. Place the paddle parallel to the water with the blade aft. If you now rotate your whole body, your blade will point forward on the opposite side of the bow, as shown in figure 12. Keep the paddle shaft parallel with the water surface and forcefully "shovel" water under the bow with short strokes powered by body rotation. This parallel-to-the-water cross draw is a powerful stroke and works exceptionally well in shallow water.

After it is mastered, try lifting the upper hand farther away from the surface. The blade will now go deeper, but the recovery will be more difficult. This high cross draw is good for "planting" the blade in one position for an extended time, such as when moving the bow out into swift water when coming out of an eddy. The high cross draw turns into a cross high brace if the blade is placed "on" the water away from the boat with the shaft slanting toward the center of the boat. The distinction between a high draw and a brace is merely a matter of angle.

Figure 12.   The cross bow draw. The grip arm is held with the elbow tucked in close, while the shaft arm is stiff and fully extended. Power is applied by rotating the trunk and moving the blade toward the bow.

Figure 13.   The stern pry is done with the paddle shaft almost parallel to the water. The grip arm is fully extended with the grip far out over the water at the start. The shaft arm is bent at the elbow and tucked against the trunk to act as a fulcrum. Power is applied by a short trunk rotation. Held in a fixed position, this is a rudder stroke.

Stern Pry and Reverse Sweep. To push the stern away from the paddle requires some form of pry stroke. The easiest is the stern pry. In this stroke the paddle is almost parallel to the water. start "learning" with the paddle blade straight back and perpendicular to the water. The elbow of the lower or fulcrum hand is held in close behind the trunk while the upper hand reaches out over the water. The power comes from a short rotation of the shoulders above the waist. Tuck the blade far under the stern at the start and continue only a little past dead astern. Do not continue forward into a reverse sweep unless you want the resulting backward force on the boat. The straight up and down pry that is used in the bow may also be used in the stern; however, it is not a good shallow water stroke and it applies force farther forward, which is less desirable.

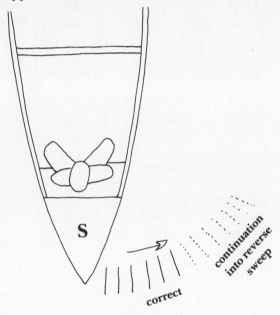

Figure 14. *Path of the paddle in the stern pry. Continuation of this stroke into a boat-slowing reverse sweep is a common mistake.*

RUDDER STROKES

The rudder is a familiar part of most ships and boats, and most people are aware of the way a rudder pushes the stern of a moving boat to one side. It is less obvious that a paddle, especially in the hands of a bow paddler, can act the same way as a conventional rudder.

23

The most important requirement for rudder action is motion of the craft with respect to the water. There can be no rudder action without *relative* motion. Moving *in* a fast current is not enough, but moving faster than the current works fine.

The second requirement is that the paddle blade be placed so that it makes an angle with respect to this relative motion. For the sternman this angle seems obvious when he is moving forward, but after a turn is initiated, the angle may not be correct for increasing the turn if the back of the canoe is slipping sideways, since the relative angle of the paddle to the moving water is now less.

So long as the angled blade is planted near the end of the boat, it does not matter which end. Bow rudder strokes are not just "allowed"; they are effective. Often the bowman spots an obstacle first and can initiate a turn faster than he could communicate to the stern in any other way. It is especially important in the bow that the paddle be held at a fixed angle as long as the rudder action is wanted. For instance, a single "fixed" (no motion of the paddler) draw stroke correctly placed to create the desired angle is far more effective than several draws with paddle motion incorrectly placed. Correct placement of rudder strokes is discussed below.

Bow Rudder on the Paddler's Own Side. The bow rudder is developed by modifying the draw stroke. Place the paddle in the water vertically in the draw position close to the side of the boat. Now move the stroke aft until the blade makes an angle with the boat direction. Finally move just the blade forward somewhat and the upper hand down and in a bit. The result is the bow rudder draw stroke shown in figure 15. This is a very powerful position and will bring a fast-moving boat about quickly.

The duffek stroke is also effective in the bow as a rudder but it is more difficult to hold. The draw described above can be gradually turned into a duffek sweep as the force on the blade is reduced by the boat's coming about in the turn. The duffek sweep is described fully as a solo paddling stroke. Master the draw stroke rudder first.

Figure 15.   Draw strokes used for ruddering. Note the backward braking angle on the bow paddle and also the angle of the paddler's body.

Bow Rudder on the Off-Paddle Side. A cross bow draw is an ideal bow rudder stroke. It is easy to hold the blade at an angle well forward even when the boat is moving fast. The low horizontal cross bow (figure 16) is preferred in shallow water, but many paddlers like to raise the upper hand somewhat to produce a stroke that is less horizontal but easier to hold for several seconds while the boat responds.

Stern Rudder Strokes. The sternman is restricted to strokes on one side of the boat. Motion toward the paddle side requires the same rudder draw as is used by the bow paddler. In the stern, place this stroke as far aft as possible. The sternman in figure 15 is using this stroke.

To move toward the other side, use the stern pry. The correct angle is particularly important here; 20-40° is good. Figure 16 shows the stern pry position before the angle has been applied to the paddle, while figure 17 shows a side view.

Figure 16. Low cross bow used as a rudder. The sternman is in position for a stern pry but has not yet changed the angle of the blade with respect to the boat.

Figure 17. Stern pry used as a rudder. Note how the elbow of the lower arm is tucked in.

How Much Rudder Angle Is Right — Practice Will Tell.
Avoid too much angle at the beginning of a rudder stroke. A
large angle will slow the boat down excessively and will tend to
wrench the shoulder muscles. As the stroke takes hold increase
the angle.

To practice rudder strokes, paddle forward fast on still
water. Suddenly apply the rudder stroke and see what happens. With a little practice a single rudder action will be able to
turn the boat 90° or more in a short distance. Practice having
the bowman initiate the turn, with the sternman "reading" the
bowman and following almost instantaneously with his own
rudder stroke.

Slithering. The most important rock dodging technique is
called the *slither*. The slither is best described as: change direction, paddle ahead, change direction. For the paddlers it involves paddling faster than the current and then executing the
following sequence: rudder, paddle ahead, rudder. Practice
this sequence on calm water until it is mastered.

BACK PADDLING

Moving a canoe backward is often just as important as
going forward. Back paddling is rarely done for long; but
while it is, strength and effectiveness are called for. For instance, imagine coming around a bend only to be confronted
with a fall immediately ahead. No time to turn around! Just
back paddle hard, and get to shore.

Straight Back Stroke. There are at least three back strokes
regularly used by experienced paddlers. The most powerful is
the straight back stroke (see figures 18 and 19). Start with the
trunk bent forward and the paddle horizontal with the blade
almost flat on the water behind. The grip hand must be out
over the water, which will require stretching the corresponding arm far forward with shoulder forward and down. The
shaft arm is bent at the elbow just enough so the stroke does not
start underwater. Power is applied by straightening the body

27

up. The arms stay relatively straight, with rotation of the shoulders and trunk doing the work.

It is most important that the blade track straight forward alongside the boat, with the blade angle perpendicular to the direction of motion. Blade angle is often a problem with this stroke. The grip hand wrist must be cocked with the thumb down slightly or the blade will push the boat sideways.

Figure 18.   Back stroke viewed from in front.

The second key point is the path of the grip hand. It must stay out over the water. It if comes in front of the paddler's chest, the stroke will turn into a reverse sweep with a large sideways push on the boat. This push is the most common problem causing tandem paddlers to fail when they are attempting the back paddle and set maneuver.

All of the power is delivered in the back stroke by the time the paddle is alongside. To recover drop the grip hand suddenly across the chest and then reach forward for the next stroke.

Figure 19. Back stroke viewed from the side.

A Back Stroke for Shallow Water. In very shallow water, the blade will hit bottom in a straight back stroke. Here there is no choice but to bring the grip hand inward in front of the chest. To avoid the push problem described above, the strokes should be short and out to the side. If both paddlers in a tandem boat use this stroke at the same time and correctly, the boat will track almost in a straight line; but if the stern paddler reaches too far back, the stern will be pushed sideways more strongly than it is moved backward.

Combination Back Strokes. It should be clear from the discussion above that it is no problem to combine a back stroke and a pry into a reverse sweep. It is almost impossible to do a straight back stroke so that it also acts as a draw stroke. Instead use the draw stroke but turn around as far as possible until a three-quarter or backward draw results.

29

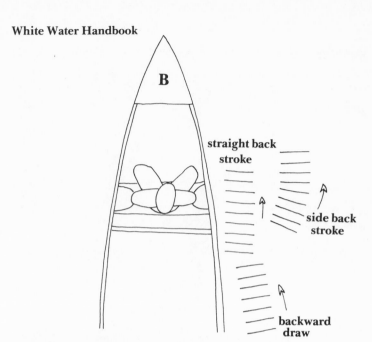

Figure 20.   The three back strokes make quite different tracks in the water. The straight back stroke turns the boat the least.

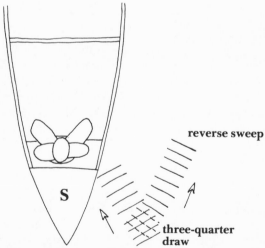

Figure 21.   Combination back strokes push the boat sideways. For some paddlers every back stroke is a reverse sweep. This is wrong. Save the reverse sweep for those times when both backward and sideward motion are desired.

BRACING STROKES AND LEANING

Braces are stabilizing strokes and are not easy to practice, since it is difficult to simulate an unstable craft except in dangerous circumstances. For instance, figure 22 shows a paddler demonstrating a low brace in still water. The arms and body are correctly placed, but the knees are not. The far knee is not even touching the boat. In an upset situation, however, the boat would be farther upon its side and the knee would be pushing it back into the upright position.

Figure 22.   The low brace. Note that both hands start out on the water.

Low Brace. In the ideal low brace both hands are over or in the water. In an open boat this is often impossible. If the grip hand is "over" the boat the blade obviously cannot lie flat on the water, but the most important aspect of the low brace is its timely application, not its style (see figures 23 and 24). Practice both kinds of low brace. For greatest effectiveness, the elbow of the shaft hand must be over the shaft in the "push up" position, as in figure 22.

Figure 23.   Here the bow paddler is using a low brace for stability in turbulent water.

Figure 24.   Low brace being used for stability by a C-1'er playing a hydraulic.

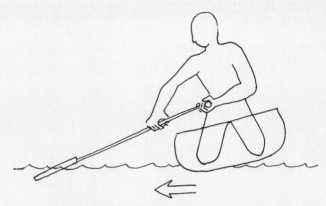

Figure 25. When performing the low brace the shaft elbow suddenly rotates forward over the shaft while the grip hand rotates palm up and drops toward the water. The current runs left to right (open arrow).

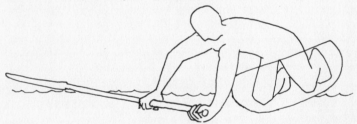

Figure 26. Here the flat of the blade gives support while the paddler rights the boat by bending at the waist and pushing with the far knee. This is an extended low brace.

Where Braces Are Needed. You need a brace whenever the water threatens to turn your boat upside down. While this can happen unexpectedly in great turbulence, it most often occurs when entering or leaving current broadside, such as when you are paddling out from the eddy behind a large rock. Figure 27 shows the sequence of events when a canoe is suddenly pushed out into a swift broadside current. The upstream bilge acts like an upside down aircraft wing. As it is pulled down by the current, the situation becomes increasingly unstable, since the hydrofoil effect increases. The transition from (A) to (C) takes only one or two seconds, even with paddlers in the boat.

33

Leaning to Counteract an Upstream "Flip." To counteract the rotation due to a crosscurrent, the paddler must lean away from the current. In (A) in figure 27, a paddler leaning to the right would place all his weight on the right side of the boat. This force would then counteract that of the current.

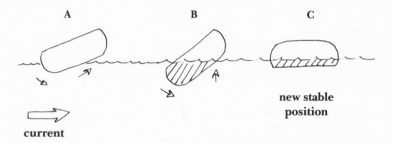

Figure 27.   Sequence of events when a boat is subjected to a sudden current from the left. In (A) the current rushing under the upstream bilge sucks this side down while buoyancy forces the downstream side up. In (B) the upstream gunwale is underwater and the boat begins to fill. The end result is (C) where some air is trapped due to the sudden upset.

There are two circumstances where a lean can be planned. When coming out from behind a rock into current at a right angle to the boat direction, the lean is always downstream. When placing the bow suddenly into still water — into an eddy behind a rock, for instance — while the momentum of the boat itself is downstream, the lean must be upstream. In this latter circumstance the boat is moving *with respect to* the still water, so the lean is away from the still water. For the expert white water paddler, correct leaning becomes instinctive.

High Brace. Figure 28 shows a paddler in a high brace. In this stroke the paddle is held as for the draw but the blade is farther from the boat so that it is "flatter" on the water. The high brace is most often used by a bow paddler on the downstream side when coming out from an eddy. It combines the action of the draw with some support while the paddler leans far out over the water.

Figure 28.   The high brace is typically used for support while leaning downstream during exit from an eddy. The powerful current from the right "attempts" to roll the boat upstream.

Figure 29.   To demonstrate this cross high brace the boat was spun rapidly. The brace is used to stop the spin.

Cross High Brace. The high cross draw can also be used as a high brace as shown in figure 29. It is used by the bow paddler coming from an eddy while paddling on the upstream side.

Both the low and the high brace are used by C-1 paddlers when playing sideways in a hydraulic. This is discussed in the chapter on solo paddling.

III

Techniques for Paddling C-1's and Open Canoes Solo

This chapter combines information on both open canoes and the decked-over slalom boats usually referred to simply as C-1's; however, the techniques and concepts applicable to the two kinds of boats are similar. The open boater works a little harder to maneuver a larger craft through the water, but the C-1'er has a more difficult time keeping upright in turbulent water. It is assumed here that the reader has mastered the material in the chapter on paddling a canoe tandem.

Where to Sit in an Open Boat. For white water a solo paddler should be near the center of an open boat. Kneeling just in front of the center thwart is good for many paddlers, since the thwart acts as a third suspension point. This position is especially recommended in a head wind. With a tail wind, a position just behind the center thwart in a high kneel with the thighs resting against the thwart is good. If the wind is strong kneeling against the rear thwart will work.

Each of the center positions has its adherents, so each paddler should try both and find which is the least tiring in any situation. Some paddlers build in elaborate seats and thigh straps. For details see the C-1 discussion in the equipment chapter.

While the discussion of strokes could begin with moving the boat forward or backward in a straight line, certain concepts common to both turning and straight-line paddling must be discussed first.

THE SWEEP CIRCLE CONCEPT

Figure 30 shows a large circle drawn with a canoeist in the center. This circle is the imaginary path made by the end of the paddle blade as the boater moves the paddle around the boat in the largest circle possible without excessively leaning forward or to the side. It is shown as a full circle, but for a right-side paddler the left rear quadrant would be missing and *vice versa* for a left paddler.

In still water, the motion of the paddle blade around or tangent to the sweep circle will tend to spin the boat in the opposite direction. When a boat is moving, a blade force tangent to the circle will turn the boat rudder fashion, even if the paddle is not moving with respect to the boat.

If the paddle is moved around a circle closer in, the effects will be reduced. If the paddle is moved toward the center of the circle, no turning of the boat will result. These are the simple facts. Real paddling is more complicated, but still worth analyzing conceptually.

The forward stroke, with the blade moving straight alongside the boat in a line parallel to the keel, will cause the boat to spin off course somewhat. Why? Consider the end of the power stroke, when the blade is next to the boat. Here the motion is tangent to a small circle drawn about the center of the boat. The circle is small so the force is small, but the motion is still tangent to a circle away from the center and turning results.

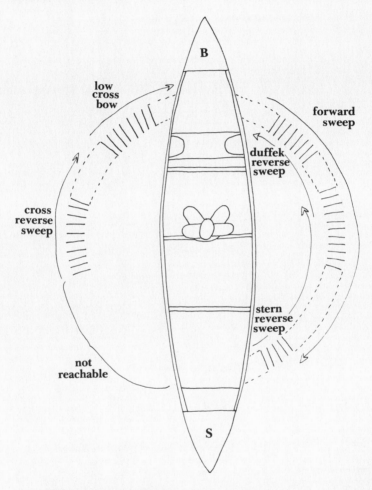

Figure 30.   The sweep circle for a right-side paddler. The circle is the farthest path the blade can sweep through the water. Effective turning strokes move the paddle blade along the circle. The major turning strokes are named here.

PADDLING STRAIGHT FORWARD

The sweep circle concept explains why a straight forward stroke along the right side of the boat will always cause the track to move somewhat to the left. It does not explain what to do to correct the situation.

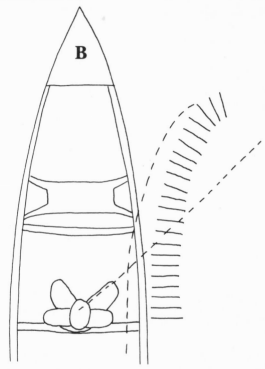

Figure 31. A short C-stroke at the beginning of the forward stroke will move the bow to the right. The C must occur early so it is not a draw stroke down the straight dotted line. If the blade tucks partway under the boat (dotted C-stroke path), the correction is more effective and the natural tendency to turn left is less.

Correction Techniques. Good paddlers modify the forward stroke so that the boat tracks in a straight line. Poor paddlers limit themselves to separate correction strokes that use more physical energy, waste time, and add drag, slowing down motion through the water. Figure 31 shows one way to modify the stroke. A toward-the-boat hook is placed at the start of the stroke. The body mechanics of this hook will be apparent after the paddler makes the duffek stroke. Avoid a wild hook that is merely a pull toward the center of the boat. A second correction is accomplished by changing the blade angle as in figure 32. Yet another helpful technique is to tuck the blade well under the boat to lessen the tendency of the bow to move left in the first place. Good paddlers combine all of these techniques, so little correction must be done at the end of the stroke.

Figure 32. Turning the blade as shown at the beginning of the forward stroke will move the bow to the right.

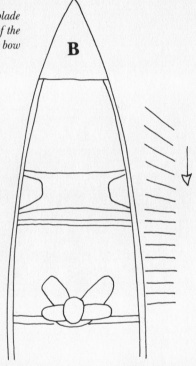

Corrections Out Behind — the J-Stroke. The J-stroke used by a stern paddler will not work solo. The push occurs too close to the center of the boat. To move the correction farther aft is not easy. Continuing the forward stroke aft beyond the midline merely "lifts" water and is inefficient. Rather, the paddler must rotate the upper wrist to the "thumb down" position while relaxing slightly. The blade will then "knife" quickly aft where an additional flick of both wrists will result in a push near the sweep circle.

By using each of the techniques discussed, the expert seems to move straight forward with little effort. With sufficient practice and attention to where to apply the paddle action, anyone can learn to do this. Mere practice of poor technique will not do. Always try to analyze why the boat responds the way it does, until good technique becomes automatic.

Figure 33.   J-stroke correction. Note cocking of wrists and the "thumb down" on the upper hand.

Stern Pry Correction. The stern pry is the most powerful correction stroke, but it takes extra time and slows down forward motion. It should be one stroke in the boater's repertory, not the only one. If the stern pry is used, it works best as a separate stroke placed as far aft as possible. For instance, three forward strokes might be followed by one stern pry. Done near the center of the boat, a pry will have only one effect; the boat will slow down and move slightly sideways. Place the pry far back.

PADDLING BACKWARD

The straight back stroke has the same problem as the forward stroke. Since the blade cannot be made to pass directly under the keel, there will always be some change of course imparted to the boat which must be corrected.

Back J-Stroke. The most elegant correction for the back stroke is analogous to the J-stroke described in the previous chapter. Make a back stroke in the usual way. When the blade is alongside, relax and rotate both wrists outwards (clockwise for a right-side paddler), so that the blade is free to knife forward toward the bow. Just before the blade leaves the water, the shaft hand (which is now well forward) gives a push while the grip pulls.

Figure 34.   Stern pry correction. The thumb of the upper hand is up.The blade is placed in the water far behind the paddler.

43

Cross-Over Corrections. The easiest correction when paddling backward is the low cross bow draw. It uses strong body
muscles, and if it is started a bit farther aft than usual it
contributes to backward motion. The cross back stroke (done
next to the boat) and the cross reverse sweep can also be used,
but they take too much time and place the body in an awkward
position. Where the back J-stroke won't do, use the cross bow.

Figure 35. The cross back stroke is placed as close to the boat as possible.

Backward Draw. It is easy for the open boater to rotate to face
aft, and even the strapped-in C-1'er can rotate a surprising
amount. The backward draw (from back to front) is particularly appropriate when one wants to reach back into an eddy or
other patch of water which is moving at a different speed than
the water seen by the rest of the boat. Slalom racers often start a
backward motion with this stroke, then shift hand position
partway through to the straight back stroke followed by the
reverse-J. (Ability to combine strokes in this way is the sign of
an expert.)

TURNING STROKES

The most effective turning strokes move the blade tangentially *around* the sweep circle either forward or in the reverse direction. No one body position is effective for the whole circle, however; so the paddler must learn or review a number of strokes. These will be discussed one at a time, and then how to select the correct turning stroke will be covered.

Forward Sweep. A full sweep is done with the paddle shaft almost horizontal. Lean forward just a little at the start with the shaft arm fully extended but with the wrist cocked. The grip hand is in front of the chest. Power is supplied by body rotation. The first part of the sweep is most effective and is often ignored by the novice paddler. Vary the distance of this stroke from the center of the boat for more or less turning action. Most novice paddlers do a slight sweep instead of a true straight forward stroke.

Cross Bow. The cross bow draw might be more correctly called the cross bow reverse sweep when done by the solo paddler. This stroke is most often used to turn suddenly toward the off-paddle side. Its rudder action does not slow the boat very much.

Figure 36. The cross reverse sweep requires that the shaft hand choke up on the shaft. Power is applied by rotating the trunk.

Cross Reverse Sweep. To get more braking action into a cross stroke, choke up farther with the shaft hand so the blade dips into the water far out from the side and well back. Rotation is all done with body muscles.

Reverse Sweep. To move all the way from the stern to the bow on the paddler's side requires two separate strokes whose effective range overlaps out to the side. No one position of arms and hands is optimum for traversing the full half circle. To do a reverse sweep, start in the stern pry position and rotate the body until the paddle is far out to the side. Do not attempt to use this stroke forward of the beam, since the arms are no longer positioned for good effect.

Figure 37. The duffek or bow reverse sweep.

Duffek Reverse Sweep. The remarkable change in kayaking technique that came about with Duffek's invention of the stroke that bears his name also applies to solo canoeing. To get into the duffek position, hold the paddle blade out to the side at chest level with hands out front. Rotate wrists up and backward along with the elbows until the normal power side of the blade faces forward instead of aft. The thumb of the grip hand will point straight down just in front of one's face. Finally lower the shaft elbow until its forearm is horizontal. Figure 37 shows a paddler in the duffek position, while figure 38 shows the path of the stroke. It is possible to reach quite far back with this stroke, but great care should be taken and under no circumstances should the grip hand be placed behind the head. This extreme position is an invitation to a dislocation of the shoulder. When learning this stroke, start it halfway between alongside and the bow.

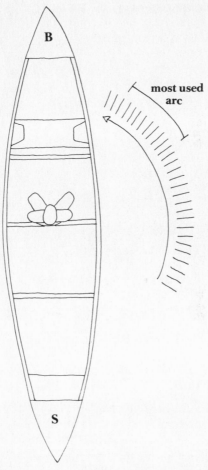

Figure 38. The duffek stroke is used along the path shown here. It can be taken as a complete stroke, but most often the canoeist selects only part of the path shown.

Cross Bow Forward Stroke. This valuable stroke was once thought to be beyond the pale. Now it is seen often. It is a very short stroke done close to the bow near the sweep circle. It is almost a series of bounces off the surface of the water. It is listed here along with the turning strokes, since it is most often used with the blade angled as shown in figure 39. Its most common use is to help keep the boat in an eddy by checking excessive spin at the end of an eddy turn.

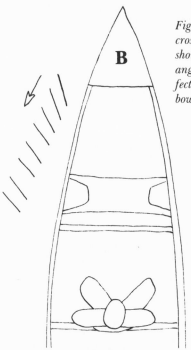

Figure 39. Not only is the cross bow forward stroke very short, but it is often done with an angled blade as shown so the effect is opposite that of the cross bow draw.

WHICH TURNING STROKE IS BEST

Without changing paddle sides one can do either forward or reverse strokes almost anywhere three-quarters of the way around a circle. Which stroke position is best depends upon conditions. Not only may the boat be moving ahead or astern with respect to the water, but local conditions vary from point to point. Placing the paddle in the still water of an eddy is entirely different in its effect than a stroke in swift current.

In white water you will usually be moving faster than the water. You can use this forward momentum to great advantage when initiating a turn. Where you place your paddle will not only determine which direction you turn but will also affect whether the center of the boat gets closer to or farther from the side of the river toward which you are turning. For instance, compare the stern reverse sweep with the duffek stroke placed out to the side and forward. In figure 40 both would alter the boat's heading toward the right, but the effects of the two strokes are not the same. The stern reverse sweep pushes the stern to the left and also moves the paddler left a little. The bow tends to be the pivot point. The boat does not slow down much.

original track   **original track**

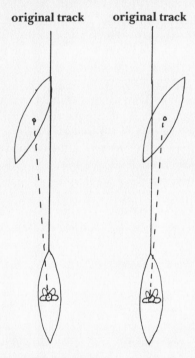

Figure 40. Two strokes for turning right while moving forward are compared. In (a) the stern reverse sweep moves the center of the boat left. In (b) the duffek or side and front reverse sweep moves the center of the boat to the right. The difference in the side to side location of the paddler can be over six feet, so choice of the correct turning stroke makes a big difference.

49

Now consider the duffek; here, the paddle tends to slow the boat down as the boat pivots about its center. As the stroke is continued around the sweep circle toward the bow, the bow is moved more and more to the right. If you want to turn into an eddy on your right, this is the preferred stroke when the whole boat must move closer to the rock. If you are already too close, the stern reverse sweep will help get the boat away from the rock a little while the turn is taking place.

In many situations the duffek can be brought around to the bow during an eddy turn in just the time required for the boat to turn broadside. Without taking the paddle from the water, you can then continue into a forward stroke to drive the bow into the still water in the eddy.

For the right-hand paddler to do an eddy turn on the left requires similar paddle placement on the cross-over side. The same combined stroke is also possible here. Start with a full cross reverse sweep and move the paddle around the sweep circle toward the bow, where the arms will be in the low cross bow position. Finish off by continuing the paddle around for a short cross bow forward. Or, if you wish, lift the paddle across the bow for a conventional forward stroke.

There is no stroke on the cross-over side that has the same effect as the stern reverse sweep on the paddle side.

LEANING AND BRACING SOLO

The solo paddler uses the same leans and braces as are used tandem; however, all maneuvering must be done from the center of the boat. Thus, the braces in particular must be modified so they help turn the boat as well as stabilize it.

Critical Lean Angle. Almost without exception novice paddlers are afraid to lean their boat up on its side. An important feature of every boat is its critical angle of lean. An open boat can usually be tipped all the way until water comes over the gunwales before it will fail to right itself.

C-1'ers should explore how far over they can lean the boat with a spotter standing in shallow water. The boater keeps his body vertical while bending at the waist. At the same time the spotter rotates the boat up on its side. Even with the paddler strapped in place, the critical angle is almost ninety degrees. It soon becomes apparent that what is important is not the angle of the boat but where the paddler has his weight.

Stay Loose in the Hips. When the expert enters a stretch of wild and turbulent water he keeps loose about the hips. The boat is allowed to rock from side to side with the ever changing surface of the water while the torso remains essentially vertical. A good exercise to get one started reacting the right way is to hold your paddle overhead. Then rock the boat from side to side with the hips. You should be able to get the boat almost up on its sides at the high points of each motion.

Low and High Brace. To learn the correct body and hand positions for the low brace and the high brace, reread the appropriate sections in the previous chapter. Here concentration will be on how and where to use these strokes.

Leaving and Entering Eddies. When leaving an eddy with a peel out or downstream turn, the bow needs to catch the downstream current while the stern is held by the still water. In addition a downstream lean is required. Begin by driving the bow up on to the swift water in the chute coming past the rock. Then do a forward high brace. By placing the paddle well forward, you will help spin the boat, while the brace will enable you to lean out over the water, avoiding an upstream flip. It is immaterial which side one is paddling on; the brace is always on the downstream side. A cross high bace is just as good as the on-side stroke.

When entering an eddy suddenly, the high brace is on the upstream side. The important part of the maneuver is to lean so the bottom of the boat faces the still water in the eddy. You should be able to enter a well defined eddy "paddleless" with only a lean of the proper degree. Practice this elegant technique where a spill won't cause difficulty.

Playing in Holes. Nothing is better for developing balance and reflexive responses than playing in holes. Figure 41 shows a C-1'er in the hydraulic below a shallow ledge. He is leaning on a high brace which is supported by the high speed underwater jet. The arms are quite close to the body. In this position a flick of the wrists will shift to the low brace position. While a low brace will get the paddler back upright from an almost upside down position, only a high brace will allow the paddler to escape the hole.

Figure 41. The high brace is used here for support while playing in a hydraulic. There is a strong underwater current moving from right to left. The current at the surface is left to right. To escape from the hole the paddler will angle the blade slightly to pull the boat forward or back.

Escaping from a Hole. The grip hand is all important in getting out of a hydraulic. By changing the blade angle you can make the blade pull the boat forward or back. One should work to the bow or stern end of the hole, where with a little luck the boat can be brought around to line up with the current. The center of a hydraulic is its lowest point. Often one can work backward but not quite out, then forward to the center of the hole where the forward momentum plus the proper blade angle is enough to come out the forward end.

Playing is not just for C-1's. Open boaters must be more careful of where they play, but they will also sharpen their skills. Many top solo open boaters use the decked C-1 to improve their skills.

ESKIMO ROLLS IN A CANOE

It goes without saying that only the decked plastic C-1- and C-2-style canoes can be rolled. An open boat with adequate flotation is too stable and broad of beam to roll when upside down. Rolling a C-2 requires that at least one paddler learn the C-1 roll, so this roll will be discussed first.

There are three phases to the C-1 roll: the setup, the pull phase, and the push phase. The setup is easy to learn, since one can get into position before doing a practice flip-over.

Setup. The most important aspect of the setup is the body and head position. The body is forward on the deck with the head face down. Persons who habitually tilt their head back when rolling can be identified by the scars on their face and forehead. Let the helmet contact any rocks while you are upside down. That is what it's for.

Throughout the roll the hands hold the paddle as they would in a forward stroke. It is a great mistake to let the hands slip to some other position on the paddle during the setup. Identify in your mind which side of the blade is the power face in the forward stroke. You need to keep this in mind during the other phases.

While still upright lean forward on the deck with the power face of the blade up. The shaft arm is extended with the wrist cocked, while the grip is held at about chin level by a bent arm tucked in close to the body. (If you take a forward stroke immediately before the setup and "glue" your shaft hand to the shaft, you will *have* to cock your wrist correctly.) You must memorize the setup position so well that it can be acquired when you are upside down after a spill.

Pull Phase. The pull phase seems quite different to the paddler and to an observer on shore. The observer should see the blade appear forward and flat on the water at the setup. It then planes on the surface or just below until the paddle is out to the side. To the paddler it feels as if the paddle were first pushed to the side slightly with the shaft hand while the body sweeps to the upright kneel position with respect to the boat. This is a body motion. The hands move very little. Trunk motion and correct blade angle cause the blade to plane along the surface of the water. The hands stay close to the chin (grip) and just above the head (shaft).

Push Phase. The push phase is the familiar low brace. If it is not familiar, learn it first. However, at the end of the pull phase the paddler is more or less face up, while a low brace requires a face down position. The change is made by rotating the body, the hands, and the blade a half turn about the long axis. The low brace — push the shaft, pull the grip — uses a little arm muscle, but it is primarily a bending forward and to the side at the waist while the hips flip the boat upright. The hip flip precedes any attempt to lift the body out of the water. The face leaves the water last.

HINTS ON LEARNING TO ROLL A C-1

1. Learn with a spotter who can both coach and assist.

2. Try going directly from a forward stroke to the setup without moving the hands on the paddle. You will be forced to cock the shaft hand wrist correctly.

3. Have the spotter position the paddle and guide it during the pull phase.

4. Practice the hip motion without a paddle by holding

the spotter's hands underwater near the surface. Your face and chest must point toward the bottom and your head must leave the water last.

5. Practice the low brace, paying particular attention to facing the bottom, leading with the grip hand as you spill the boat, and having the head leave the water last.

6. As early as possible try to put the whole roll together into a single smooth motion, with no hesitation between its parts.

7. Never push off the bottom. If in trouble, face the bottom and rely on your spotter. Pushing off the bottom encourages facing up, a difficult habit to break and one guaranteed to prevent a successful roll. It is much easier for the spotter to right your boat if you face the bottom.

THE OFF-SIDE ROLL

People avoid the off-side roll for two reasons. First, the standard roll seems easier, perhaps because more people can do it and therefore teach it. Second, the final position has the arms crossed over like a pretzel. The fact is that this roll is essential for C-2 paddling in big water like the Grand Canyon. Further, the trunk muscles exert every bit as much righting moment on the boat up until the very end of the roll.

There are three parts to the off-side roll — the setup, the sweep, and the off-side brace. Learn this roll in a C-1 with a spotter.

Setup. Practice the setup right side up. Lean forward on the deck with the head tucked down for face protection. The arms are in almost the same position as for the standard roll, but the wrists are rotated the other way, with the non-power side of the blade up. The grip hand is palm down. As with the standard roll, go from the forward stroke to the setup with no slip in grip.

Sweep. Sweep the opposite direction from that used for a standard roll. Angle the blade to get it to track as near the surface as possible. This sweep seems all wrong to one who does the standard roll "instinctively." The sweep ends with the paddler facing the bottom.

Figure 42.   Here a C-1 paddler is falling toward the off-paddle side to practice the off-side brace, which is the last phase of an off-side roll.

Off-Side Brace. Figure 42 shows a C-1 paddler in the off-side brace position. Learn this brace by holding the paddle horizontally overhead while facing forward. The grip hand is over the head palm down and the shaft hand is out to the side where the elbow is bent ninety degrees. Fall to the off side. Leave the blade on the surface and let the boat continue upside down by a rotation of the hips so the body remains near the surface. A sudden hip snap will bring the boat up. The body is raised off the water last by continuing the natural motion of the paddle. You will end up with the shaft hand arm over your head and with the arms wound up. This brace works only if the body is near the surface. If you wait too long, you must get in the setup position for either the standard or off-side roll.

POLING THE CANOE

The setting pole, the guide's old standby for quick water, is much neglected but not obsolete. It can become an instrument of precision in many shallow and rocky streams when the water is medium or low. In dropping downstream, the pole is always used to *snub*, or check the downstream motion, and with it the canoe can be placed almost to the inch, stopped dead in midstream, or moved sideways to a new channel. In easy rapids the pole enables the canoeman to make a leisurely and controlled run; when the water is low and the river is strewn with obstructions, the pole allows an effortless and pleasurable descent where a paddler would be frustrated by scraping boat and scratching paddle. The pole is often the best, or even the only, way of ascending a stream with ease, and opens to exploration remote areas otherwise difficult of access.

The pole itself is usually straight-grained spruce about an inch and a quarter in diameter and ten to twelve feet long. Ash or maple of a somewhat smaller diameter may also be used to make a pole which is both more flexible and a bit heavier. The lower end may be fitted with a steel shoe to take the wear of a rocky bed, and the upper end should have an elongated knob to prevent it from sliding unannounced from the canoeman's hands.

An open canoe is used for poling, and for upstream work it should have good lines and be at least seventeen feet long. The shorter and stubbier canoes have insufficient way and settle back between thrusts. The pole can be used, if need be, from a kneeling position, but the ordinary position is standing, with the feet well apart on either side of the keel.

The first rule of poling, whether upstream or down, is that the downstream end of the canoe be trimmed somewhat down. For a single canoeman without duffel, this means that he may conveniently stand just behind the center thwart in ascending, and just in front of it when descending, a stream. If he has duffel, he may carry it at the bow in descending, and take a position somewhere behind the center thwart. And if he prefers the more sternward position when not carrying duffel, then he may arrange for it with some makeshift load at the bow. Better a log, which will float in the event of an upset, than a rock for this load. With the loaded end downstream, the canoe tends to stay in alignment with the current; violate this principle and despite all your efforts your canoe will turn broadside under you, with some probability of a ducking to follow. The neophyte in poling will keep his paddle close at hand to take the sting out of an error with the pole.

The technique of poling is something more to be experienced than easily analyzed. In downstream work the pole is always busy snubbing to check the forward motion from the current, and in upstream work to drive against the water. In both cases, the force applied by the pole is always in delicately opposed balance with the force of the stream on the canoe, and thus the side of the canoe opposite the pole is angled slightly toward the current. If you change sides with the pole, you must bring the upstream end of the canoe neatly up and across the line of the current as you do so, catching your new position with the pole on the other side. Hold the pole with a wide grip so that it passes the body fore-and-aft, and although you may shift at your pleasure from one side to the other to improve your hold on the riverbed or change your path, do not use the pole crossed in front of the body lest it be caught and you with it.

In poling upstream you learn rapidly to plot a crafty course where the river offers the least opposition. The edge of a current is preferable to its middle, and an eddy is better yet. You can approach a small chute from the side water of an eddy, drive up the chute with effort, and then move aside quickly into the slower water above. Like a hound following a difficult scent, you will find yourself crossing and recrossing the main current for temporary advantage.

Dropping with the pole does not have the speed and dash of running with the paddle, but it gives the satisfaction of precise control, and from it you may learn subtleties of the river's flow which will make you a better downstream canoeist as well.

IV

Kayak Paddling Techniques

Kayaking technique has been refined over the years to increase efficiency and decrease exertion. With the proper strokes and a knowledge of how to use the forces of the river, a kayaker travels in harmony with the water. Strength and luck may be substituted for these abilities on easier classes of white water, but they lack an essential ingredient, reliability. When a boater chooses to run more challenging water, every move must be reliable to the point of being reflexive. There is no time to think in big water.

The best place to learn and to master white water strokes is on flat water, whether it be a lake, a pool, or a local river. Each stroke described in this chapter should be continually practiced, especially during the non-boating months.

Warm Up before Paddling. Before getting into a boat, all kayakers should warm up. Shoulder injuries are very common in this sport and can be easily avoided by stretching and loosening the arms and shoulders. Toe touches, arm circles, shoulder and head rotations, and jumping jacks should be done until the paddler feels that all the tightness in the arm and shoulder area is gone. These exercises should be continued until you work up a light sweat.

Getting into the Boat. To enter the boat, place the paddle behind the cockpit, resting the shaft on the rear deck and the blade securely on land. Face the bow and squat next to the boat with the arms behind and grasping the paddle shaft. Using the paddle for stability, swing the foot closest to the boat into the cockpit and slide it forward slightly as shown in figure 43. Then swing the other foot in and with both legs extended, slide the feet forward while lowering yourself onto the seat.

Figure 43.   The paddle stabilizes the boat while the boater gets in.

Place the balls of your feet on the foot braces located on either side of the boat. If the foot braces are set at the proper length, you will be able to stretch your feet slightly forward and find that your knees rest securely against the upper deck. It should be a comfortable but secure "fit". If the foot braces are too close, the fit will be uncomfortably tight and circulation in the legs will be inhibited. If the fit is too loose, movements which require hip action, such as the roll, will be more difficult.

It is also important that the hips fit comfortably yet securely within the sides of the seat. When you become familiar with your boat, you may decide that a tighter seat fit is in order. Simply glue and tape foam blocks of sufficient thickness onto either side of it to prevent slipping around on the seat.

Attaching the Spray Skirt. The paddle is placed across the forward deck so that it is readily available while attaching the spray skirt. To attach the skirt, lean back and stretch the hem completely over the rear cockpit lip and up each side a couple of inches. With the grab loop in hand, lean slightly forward to secure the hem to the front lip. Finally, secure both sides. Check that the skirt is completely tight, and that the grab loop is out and available.

Where to Hold the Paddle. Use the following procedure to determine the proper place to grasp the paddle shaft. While holding the paddle on top of your head, have a friend adjust the position of your hands so that the elbow joints form right angles and the hands are equidistant from the blades as shown in figure 44. Tape the shaft to mark this position until it becomes second nature to hold the paddle there.

Figure 44.   The elbows are at right angles and the hands equidistant from the blades when the paddle is held correctly.

Control of the Paddle. The blades of a kayak paddle are set at right angles to each other to reduce wind resistance. The shaft must be rotated between strokes to position the blade for the next stroke. This is accomplished by one hand acting as the control hand, remaining firmly on the shaft throughout each stroke. Paddlers usually use their dominant hand as the control hand — i.e., a right-handed person always has a firm grip on the paddle with his right hand. The pivot hand loosens slightly during the stroke sequence when the blades are in the air, allowing the control hand to rotate the shaft within the pivot hand. The shaft of the paddle must be held firmly against the palms of both hands at all times. It is a common error for paddlers to loosen their fingers during a stroke, so that they no longer make a straight right angle to the shaft; this results in loss of paddle control.

Flat-bladed paddles can be used for either right-hand or left-hand control. Spoon-bladed paddles, however, are set differently for right- or left-hand control.

STROKES FOR MOVING FORWARD

Power Face. For the purpose of describing the strokes that follow, the term *power face* refers to the active side of the blade during a forward stroke. For a spoon-bladed paddle this is the concave face of the blade.

Forward Power Stroke. To begin the stroke, drop the power face into the water close to the bow. The lower arm should be completely extended, with the corresponding shoulder stretched forward. The upper arm is bent, with the hand at eye level. Move the paddle along the side of the boat, with the blade completely submerged, pulling with the lower arm and pushing with the upper arm. During this movement, the upper torso rotates in the direction of the stroke. The upper pushing arm should be moving at shoulder level with the hand staying at eye level and "punching" toward the bow of the boat until fully extended. The forward punch should not, however, cross the center line of the kayak. The punch and torso rotation part of the stroke bring the stronger back and shoulder muscles into play. The stroke ends when the pulling hand reaches the body and the pushing hand is completely extended. The stroke should be done in an upright position, with neither front-to-back nor side-to-side rocking of the upper body. The forward stroke diagrams (figures 45-46) demonstrate this sequence.

Figure 45.   The forward stroke just before placing the paddle. The lead arm is fully extended and the shoulder is twisted forward.

Figure 46.   Forward stroke viewed from in front. Note how the upper hand "punches" at eye level.

At the completion of the stroke, the paddle is lifted from the water next to the hip. The shaft is now rotated within the pivot hand to position the power face to enter the water toward the bow on the opposite side of the kayak.

The most common forward power stroke mistakes are: no eye-level punch, rocking the torso back and forth, pulling on the power blade before it is in the water, not pushing with the upper arm, and taking the blade out of the water beyond the hip.

Forward Sweep. The forward sweep is the most commonly used turning stroke. Not only does the sweep turn the boat, but it also moves it forward. Begin the stroke by reaching forward and placing the blade in the water close to the bow, as shown in figure 47. The hands need to be cocked slightly forward so that the power face is perpendicular to the water, facing away from the boat. Swing the blade away from the boat in a semicircular arc toward the stern. Power for the stroke is delivered primarily by a strong push of the upper arm, accompanied by a pull with the lower arm. The arms should remain below shoulder level throughout the sweep. Back and shoulder muscles increase the effectiveness of the stroke by rotating the torso as the paddle sweeps. Keep the hands low during this stroke — no more than three or four inches above deck level.

Figure 47.   The forward sweep stroke.

It is easy to modify the sweep stroke when less turn is desired. For example, it is often sufficient to use a half arc from the bow until the blade is perpendicular to the body. This will initiate a quick turn of the bow. By extending the paddle perpendicular to the body and sweeping to the stern, you will put more emphasis on propelling the boat forward while turning.

Paddling a Straight Course. Paddling a kayak in a straight line is a skill that requires hours of practice, while analyzing your course to determine what stroke modifications are suitable to your style and strength. One helpful exercise is to select a particular point on land to serve as a reference. Direct the bow toward this mark, completing the forward power stroke on one side. Quickly check your bearing in relation to that mark. If your bow is more than 10° off the mark, use a sweep stroke on the other side to return the bow to the center. The boat may again exceed the mark and require a light sweep on the other side. When the bow is close to center, use a power stroke. Since each paddler is different, there is no formula for the exact proportion between power stroke and sweep stroke. This can only be mastered through trial and error. The goal is to use primarily forward power strokes with a minimum of correction sweep strokes.

STROKES FOR MOVING BACKWARD

Reverse Power Stroke. For the reverse power stroke, rotate the torso slightly to the side while turning the wrists forward so that the non-power face of the blade is parallel to the surface of the water. With the lower hand, push the blade into the water just behind the hip, while pulling with the upper hand. As the stroke continues, the torso rotates back to the center position. The stroke ends when the lower hand is completely extended forward and the upper hand is at eye level. The blade should be close to the boat throughout the stroke. To set the blade for the next stroke, rotate to the opposite side while again pivoting the shaft to the non-power face.

Figure 48. Paddler looking over one shoulder while executing the reverse power stroke.

When paddling backward look only over one shoulder. Changing your head from side to side confuses and distorts your perspective of the course you are attempting to take.

67

Figure 49.   Start of the reverse sweep. Note that the back arm is fully extended.

Reverse Sweep. As in the reverse power stroke, rotate the body to the side to begin this stroke. Rotate the wrists slightly forward so that when the paddle is held aft and parallel to the boat the non-power face is perpendicular to the water and facing outward. Reaching back, drop the blade into the water close to the stern as shown in figure 49. With a completely straight arm, push the non-power face away from the boat in a wide arc, ending near the bow. The upper arm is flexed and pulling, and remains close to the body throughout the stroke. Like the forward sweep, the reverse sweep can be modified by using a half arc rather than a full arc.

Figure 50.   The reverse sweep slows and turns the kayak as shown in this sequence.

THE DUFFEK

The duffek is an effective turning stroke. It is used primarily following the forward sweep stroke on the opposite side for turning into eddies. The duffek snaps the kayak around and, with a change of the wrists, can evolve into a forward power stroke, providing additional control over the placement of the boat.

For the uninitiated, the position of the hands in a duffek stroke is somewhat awkward. As the stroke becomes more familiar, however, it will begin to feel natural.

The following sequence of moves will get you into the correct duffek position when first learning the stroke. For purposes of explanation, assume that the stroke is placed on the right side of the kayak. First, hold the paddle at shoulder level in front of the body. Cock both wrists back toward the body as far as possible. The right power face should now be facing forward. Maintain this wrist position and swing the left arm up and across the forehead so that the upper hand is to the right of the head. With the lower hand, reach out to the side one-and-a-half to two feet and place the blade in the water slightly forward of the body. The shaft of the paddle should be at a 45° angle to the boat and the blade perpendicular to the surface of the water. Lean slightly toward the stroke side.

When in the duffek position, rotate the shoulders to move the blade in an arc toward the bow. If you notice problems with your turn, check the blade angle and adjust it by turning your wrists. Study figures 51, 52, and 53.

To really get a feel for the duffek, it should be practiced with the boat moving forward in combination with a sweep stroke. Take a few forward strokes, then sweep on the left and duffek on the right. You should be able to turn the kayak 180° comfortably with this combination. When you have achieved some mastery of this stroke, concentrate on rotating the wrists inward when the power face reaches to bow, so that it is turned to the position for the forward power stroke.

Figure 51. The duffek stroke is here applied after the start of a turn with a sweep. Note from the turbulence of the water that the boat has already turned 90°.

Figure 52. In this sequence the fast-moving kayak is suddenly turned using the duffek stroke. In the third "frame," the blade is forward where an immediate forward stroke may be taken.

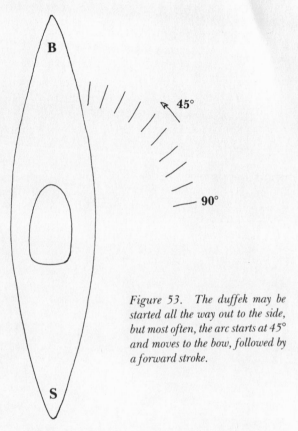

Figure 53. The duffek may be started all the way out to the side, but most often, the arc starts at 45° and moves to the bow, followed by a forward stroke.

To use a duffek for entering an eddy, begin by crossing the eddy line with a powerful far side sweep stroke, then plant the near side blade in the still or upstream water of the eddy using the duffek position. Complete the duffek stroke and, if necessary, follow through with a forward power stroke to maintain position in the eddy.

In general, with any kayak stroke where one blade is held above the head, as in the duffek, draw, and high brace strokes, care should be taken that the upper hand does not move behind the head. This position places an extreme strain on the shoulder muscles and can lead to a dislocation.

71

THE SIDE DRAW

The side draw is a correction stroke used primarily for short, rapid lateral movement, as in dodging a rock. Reach out directly to the side of the boat with the upper arm across the forehead, forming a window. With the lower arm completely extended, the power face is planted in the water two feet directly to the side of the kayak. The power face is parallel to the kayak. While leaning slightly away from the power face, pull the shaft with both arms until the blade is one to two inches from the boat.

Figure 54.   A draw stroke is used to pull the kayak sideways. Note how vertical the paddle is and that the paddler is leaning away from the draw.

THE STABILIZERS — LOW BRACES AND HIGH BRACES

Kayaks, especially in white water, react constantly to the whims of the river. The stabilizers, low braces and high braces, are a paddler's best ammunition against unsuspected upsets.

Low Brace. For a low brace, place the shaft three to four inches above the cockpit. Rotate your wrists so that the non-power face is parallel to the surface of the water. Leaning the boat, reach out as far to the side as possible with the elbows and hands over the paddle. As you push down against the shaft, the pressure of the blade on the water will support you. With a little additional pushing, you are again upright.

Figure 55. Demonstration of the low brace in still water. Note how the elbow of the brace hand is almost over the paddle shaft.

The low brace is excellent to use when playing in holes. By moving the brace toward the stern and changing the angle to a slight climbing angle, the low brace easily converts to a reverse sweep. Since the hands are low, it can just as easily be moved forward to convert to a forward sweep.

High Brace. The high brace is similar to the duffek. The hand position is the same, with the upper arm across the forehead and the lower arm extended perpendicular to the side of the body. The bracing action occurs when the power face is pulled down and toward the boat along the surface of the water. The upper arm pushes the shaft while the lower arm pulls down. As soon as resistance with the water is felt, force the knee on the leaned side against the deck. This hip snap, in combination with the brace, will bring you right up. A skilled paddler can lean a shoulder all the way into the water and then brace up. Normally the high brace is used to counteract a current from the opposite side of the boat, such as when coming out of an eddy.

Figure 56. Here a high brace is used for stability while playing a hydraulic. The current moves from left to right. Note how the elbow is directly under the wrist on the brace side.

Figure 57. The high brace is combined with a "backward draw" while the boater attempts to get out of a hole. This position with the arms behind the head risks a dislocated shoulder. A low brace and reverse sweep would be a better choice.

74

THE ESKIMO ROLL

One of the most rewarding moves in kayaking is a good roll. If possible learn to roll with the help of an experienced paddler as coach. This mentor can not only critique your progress but can also provide the physical support needed to practice the movements of a roll. Everyone learns the roll at his own pace, and every individual has his own particular rough spots. A helper can identify these spots and assist in overcoming them.

Since the roll is a combination of a number of different coordinated body motions, the following discussion gives ways to practice and achieve these individual motions before pulling them together for the actual roll.

Wet Exit. If you have never done a wet exit from your boat, or if you have but found it to be a nasty experience, you should work on wet exits with your helper. The goal is to achieve a smooth, controlled underwater exit from the boat. First, while sitting in the boat with the skirt secured, check that the grab loop is out and available. Then, concentrate on the rule that whenever you go over, you lean forward close to the deck. Look at the deck, not "up." Take a deep breath and turn the boat over, using your hips. Now, in the upside down tucked position, pull the grab loop and roll forward, your bottom emerging first, followed by your legs. Problems usually occur when paddlers, in a slight panic, try to come out to the side or back, catching their legs on the cockpit. If you are feeling at all nervous, work on keeping calm by repeating the wet exit. As you achieve control, try holding your position for five seconds before ejecting. You will soon learn that you have plenty of time to hang around under the boat.

Underwater Orientation. The first mystery of rolling is orienting yourself underwater. To work on this, have a helper stationed next to you. Turn over *away* from the helper, whose hands should be extended under the boat. Look for his hands and hold on so he can pull you up. Practice this several times, going over on one side and coming up on the other. Next, have your helper hold a paddle shaft for you to reach rather than his hands.

Hip Snap — "Knee Drive." Hip snap is essential to a successful roll, and it must become a reflexive action. Kayakers often describe how they "wear their boats." This hip snap movement embodies that concept. A good preparatory exercise is to rock the kayak from side to side while holding the body vertical. This is done by driving the knees alternately toward the opposite shoulder and thereby pushing up against the deck.

Figure 58.   The coach is teaching the hip snap. A boater must be able to right the craft with a sudden snap of the hips before the roll can be taught successfully.

Another way to practice the hip snap in preparation for rolling is to have a helper grasp your hands while you lean the boat over on its side as shown in figure 58. Now, drive the knee on the low side of the boat. Keep your head down throughout this hip snap. Your body should follow only after the boat is upright. If the hip action is correct, you will feel the boat snap back up. Increase your lean incrementally, always concentrating on the snap. When you are placing very little pressure on the helper's hands, you have a good hip snap. If you have difficulty keeping your head down, concentrate on watching your helper's feet. Don't lose sight of them until the boat is up.

As you learn to roll, you will become more familiar with the "feel" of each move. If you are having trouble with your roll later or if the roll is slow or strained, the hip snap is probably at fault. Practice the hip snap with a helper, or alongside a pool, or use the shallow area alongside a beach by pushing off the bottom.

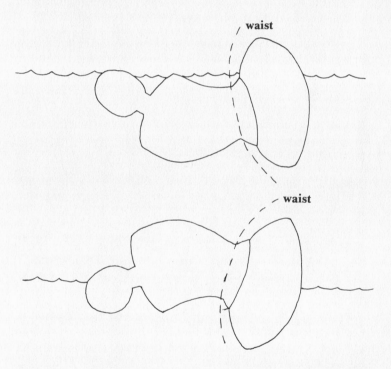

Figure 59. The hip snap is a sudden movement at the waist from the first position above to the second. Note that at the end of the hip snap the head is still underwater but the deck is essentially upright. Here the arms are omitted to emphasize the fact that all the action comes from the trunk muscles.

Setup. The setup is a paddle-holding position with respect to the boat that is learned while the boat is upright and held while the boat upsets. Later, this position must be so "instinctive" that it can be achieved underwater on the river after an unexpected spill.

The easiest roll to learn is the extended paddle roll. It requires moving the hands along the shaft to maximize the extension of the paddle for increased leverage. Do not stop when the extended roll is mastered; go on to learn the screw roll.

Most paddlers learn to roll on their dominant hand side. Bring the paddle to the side of the boat with this hand closest to the bow, and with the paddle lying along the deck. Slide your hands down the shaft so that the forward hand is about half-way down the shaft and the rear hand is on the blade. The rear hand grasps the blade at the lower corner as shown in figure 60.

Figure 60.   Setup for an extended paddle roll. Note that the lower arm lies diagonally across the blade and that the upper wrist is cocked.

This hand must be at the corner, not at the end, of the blade, so that the lower arm rests diagonally across the blade. Rotate the forward wrist away from the body. It is important that the rear blade be tight against the rear arm. Check that the forward blade is parallel to the surface of the water.

Positioning the Paddle Underwater. Your helper should position himself on the side where you will surface for this exercise. Holding the paddle in the setup position with a good forward lean, flip the boat away from the helper. Continue around underwater until the paddle nears the surface and then push it out of the water. When it is above the surface, your helper should grab it and pull you up. Practice this until there is no difficulty in knowing that the paddle is out of water.

Blade Angle. A roll uses the planing action of the paddle blade as it sweeps along the surface of the water. Therefore, proper blade angle is essential. Often, when a kayaker turns over from the setup position, the wrists will rotate a bit so that when the paddle is lifted out of the water the blade is no longer parallel to the surface.

Starting from setup position, flip over and push the paddle out of the water. Pull down on the shaft with the forward hand so that the blade contacts the water. If the blade angle is correct, the blade will slap the water. If not, it will dive. Should the paddle dive, cock your forward wrist so that you force the rear blade tight against the lower arm. Now, try another slap. It helps to keep your eyes on the forward blade to check this angle. (Diving masks can be very useful for this.) If the wrist adjustment is still confusing, have your helper turn the blade to the correct angle once you have pushed it above the surface. While he does this, concentrate on what happens to your forward wrist.

Sweep. The motion of the paddle in the roll is the same as in the forward sweep, only it is done from an upside down position. The sweep begins at the bow and follows an arc away from the boat toward the stern. The sweep is practiced from a modified setup position. Have your helper hold you under the shoulder opposite your setup side as shown in figure 61. Hold the paddle in the extended position. Lean the boat up on its side and reach out to sweep, adjusting the angle of the blade with your wrist so that it is parallel to the surface of the water. Now, slap the water and sweep out away from the boat. Watch the blade and rotate your body as it follows this course. If your blade did not dive, you are back in an upright position with very little assistance from your helper. Practice this stroke with increasing leans, until you can do it with your shoulder touching the water.

Figure 61.   Here the coach is teaching the subject to sweep the paddle with the extended paddle grip. The blade must plane along the surface without diving.

Once you have accomplished a successful sweep and have a good feel for it, begin to use the hip action discussed earlier. When the sweep has reached about 30° on its path, drive your knee. The combination of hips and a good sweep will bring you up with very little effort or strain.

Roll. Your helper should be positioned just behind the cockpit, on the opposite side from that used for the other exercises so that he can reach across the hull and pull you up.

Return to the setup position with the sharply cocked wrist and the rear blade resting tightly against the rear lower arm. It is time to put all the pieces together. First, set up and take a deep breath. Turn over, force the paddle out of the water and check the blade angle. Now, slap and sweep in a wide arc away from the boat, keeping your head down until the boat is upright. The forward arm must remain completely extended throughout the stroke; otherwise, the blade will dive.

It would be unusual for the first attempt to be successful. Don't be discouraged. There are many pieces to remember, and it is easy to lose a couple of parts along the way. The most frequent mistakes at this point are: (1) losing the blade angle, thereby causing the paddle to dive, (2) uncertainty as to the path of the sweep stroke, and (3) failure to snap the hips. To correct the blade angle problem, return to the exercise where your helper adjusts the angle after you have brought the paddle out of the water. He can then swing the blade in its proper path, while you concentrate on the changes in style you must make to duplicate this motion. Work with your helper to analyze any other problems you may be having. Try to work on them one at a time. If necessary, go back to the exercises to reinforce the hip action, the sweep stroke, or the setting of the blade angle.

River Roll. Your first roll is a triumph and should be treated as such. However, it is only the beginning. You will want to work toward a river roll, also known as a combat roll, where you turn over unexpectedly and must set up underwater. One way to practice for this is to paddle forward several strokes and then turn over while holding the paddle in only one hand. By feel, move your hands along the shaft until you can find setup position. Push the paddle out of the water, slap, sweep, and knee drive. To simulate the confusion of white water, have your helper turn you over from behind with no warning as to the side or the timing four or five times consecutively.

Figure 62.   Setup for the screw roll. The hands are held in the same position on the shaft as for paddling.

Screw Roll. The optimum roll for white water is the short paddle or *screw roll*, as it is quick to set up and flows naturally from the paddling position. You can gradually move your hands to this position. Start by placing your rear hand at the neck of the shaft and your forward hand just below its normal handhold. The forward wrist should be cocked outward to insure a proper blade angle. This position must be maintained throughout the sweep stroke. Having limited the extension of the sweep by shortening the paddle, you must emphasize a long, extended forward arm during the sweep. Your body should reach out to the side with the paddle. After you have had success in holding the paddle at the neck, then move your hands closer to the short paddle position which is shown in figure 62. Continue to work on the roll until the screw roll is mastered. Do not be satisfied with an extended paddle roll.

THE ENGLISH GATE FOR SMOOTH WATER PRACTICE

In running a complex rapid, and even more in slalom, you must match your paddling patterns to those of the river's currents and obstructions. Each stroke prepares for the next in balance, movement, and position. The overall sequence is in continuous readjustment to fit the demands of the river as they are revealed one after another ahead of you. Two complementary skills are involved — handling the boat and dealing with the water. By mastering the first in smooth water you can prepare yourself for rapid progress in the second.

A successful device for smooth water practice consists of a fixed series of maneuvers performed with respect to a slalom gate — a pair of poles spaced 36 inches apart, suspended so that their lower ends hang only a few inches above the surface. This series was called the wiggle test by the English kayakers who devised it, but is known in this country as the English gate. That it is an effective training device when intensively used has been shown by the fact that, of a small group of paddlers who used it for their only initial training, three placed very near the top of their first season of slalom competition.

The sequence is as follows:

Phase 1. Forward through the gate, a right turn, forward through again, a left turn, and forward again through the gate.

Phase 2. Reverse (backward) outside on the right, roll to left, forward through, reverse outside on the left, roll to right, and forward through the gate.

Phase 3. Reverse down the left side, reverse right turn, reverse through the gate, reverse left turn, reverse through gate.

Phase 4. Forward up the right side, roll to left, reverse through the gate, forward up the left side, roll to right, reverse through gate.

83

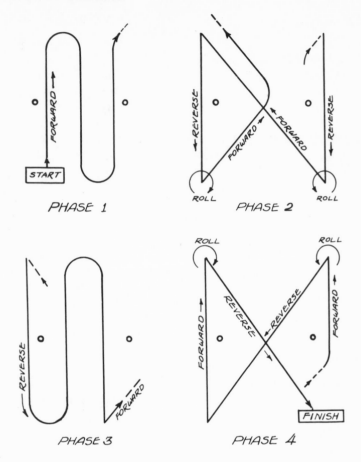

Figure 63. The four phases of the English gate sequence.

An easily portable version of the gate can be made with anchored buoys and an underwater spacer. A gate can be set over moving water for more intensive practice. Several paddlers can join in a friendly competition with the use of a stopwatch; begin timing when the bow first passes through the gate, and end it as the boat completes its last passage of the gate. Some experts can finish the sequence without touching a pole in less than 90 seconds; a paddler who has broken 120 seconds is well on his way toward mastery of his boat.

V

Running the River

The art of white water boating lies in a quick and accurate appraisal of the water ahead and in committing yourself to action. You do not oppose the river's force with your own, for you must lose; instead, you meet the river's challenge with skill. You may never forget that the tactics of the moment must be consonant with a larger strategy, for many a trap has an inviting entrance. You must know what the river can do for you and with you, and you must know what you can do with your boat and do it decisively.

HANDLING THE BOAT

Good control of the boat in quick water means placing it well for what is to come. You may need to move to the side a half a foot or twenty. One stroke may be needed, or a protracted maneuver, or a continuous set of variations, as in the tortuous path through a boulder patch. The principles of successful paddling apply to any white water boat — single kayak, single canoe, or double canoe. The double canoe, however, has a further element — the necessity for rapport between two full partners who feel themselves always to have a single purpose and who are constantly aware that each stroke not only moves the canoe but acts to pivot it about the middle as well. This and the fact that neither paddler has effective control over the entire canoe makes close cooperation essential; such cooperation will be closest when each person is experienced in both bow and stern.

Three Ways to Move Sideways. When you must move to one side, you can do so in one of three ways — by turning the bow toward that side while moving forward, by turning the stern to that side while backpaddling, and by drawing or prying the boat directly toward that side. The last is the least efficient, since the boat is much more resistant to being dragged sideways than to being moved forward or backward, yet this method is frequently necessary or useful for making abrupt but short changes in position. You will find yourself using all these methods in appropriate circumstances. In following sections we will examine some of the conditions and techniques for their use.

Staying Lined Up with the Current. Particularly where you must run a shifty course through obstructions, keep aware of the direction of the current and of your degree of alignment with it. When completely aligned you are best prepared for maneuvering, and least vulnerable to countercurrents and obstructions. The two consequences of being out of alignment, both sometimes astonishingly swift, are broaching and broadsiding on a rock.

Controlling Boat Angle in Current. As you move down a river, you are in currents whose velocity and direction are constantly changing. The flow accelerates past a constriction, then slows again. Below each obstruction is an eddy of quiet or upstream-moving water. These velocity changes can be very abrupt, especially at the boundary line of an eddy, at the bottom of a short, fast chute, or where the rush of water over a ledge meets the slower and deeper pool below. In such a place the two ends of the boat are in currents of quite different velocities. If you are out of alignment with the current here, the forces at bow and stern can spin the boat rapidly broadside and make it vulnerable to any rocks as well as to the capsizing effects of the currents.

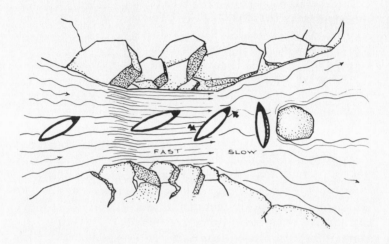

Figure 64. A boat out of alignment with the current broaching at the bottom of a chute.

Getting broadside to the waves is called *broaching,* and it can happen quite abruptly. A broached boat is much more vulnerable to rocks and obstructions. When there are no obstructions, however, being broadside to the river is neither good nor bad.

Negotiating Obstructions. There is a further hazard which may be incurred by being out of alignment. You may be caught out of position too close to an obstruction. Also, when you are not going where your boat is aimed, it seems to be easier to misread the exact direction of the current; this can lead you straight into difficulties.

In any close maneuvering, consider where the center of the boat will go, not the end you are in. The bowman in a double canoe may forget that the rest of his boat will not necessarily follow him, and, like the beginning driver who neglects the path of the rear wheels when he turns, will guide only his bow past an obstruction or into a chute. The hard-pressed stern paddler must then set things right, if he can. The bow should understand that he may need to help his partner after his own end of the boat has passed the obstruction. Another way the bow can harass his partner is by waiting too long, when approaching a rock, to pull his end over. The stern may then be unable to follow in time to prevent broadsiding.

Keeping the alignment of the double canoe is primarily the task of the stern. But let him not be too assiduous in this, for a rigidly kept alignment with the current is, at best, a tiring exercise. A boulder-strewn drop requires a snaky course, with both bow and stern bending their way around the obstacles, and a stern who keeps his alignment like an article of faith will make it more difficult for his partner to guide his end of the canoe into the chosen course. The paddler in a single canoe or kayak will more quickly gain the sense of maneuvering with least effort; in a double canoe each paddler may not be so aware of the difficulties he can make for his partner.

Slithering around Obstructions Tandem. When a boat approaches a rock or obstruction head-on, there is a sequence of strokes for getting a tandem canoe around it with dispatch. Usually the bow paddler notices the obstruction first and initiates the maneuver with a draw or pry stroke. The stern paddler "reads" the action of the bow and uses the *same* stroke. These two strokes spin the boat the same way to a new heading. Both paddlers then drive the boat ahead until they are sure that the course will clear the rock. Finally, both paddlers do a single stroke to align the boat with the current again. The sequence is called a *slither,* and slithering is the best way to negotiate a complex boulder field.

Running through Haystacks. A particular exception to the general principle of keeping alignment occurs in a long, uniform drop with plenty of water. This type of drop will produce a series of big standing waves — *haystacks* — throughout its length and at its bottom. In running straight with an open canoe, the bow will plunge head-on into these, taking on water with each. If, however, you quarter the waves by coasting down at a moderate angle to them, the canoe will rise better to each wave and less water will be taken aboard. To quarter the waves, merely turn the boat about one-quarter broadside to the current. This is the white water adaptation of the flat water canoeist's principle of avoiding paddling directly into high waves on large bodies of water.

In short chutes with a few big haystacks at the bottom, a decked canoe or kayak can be paddled forward to plunge straight through, with bracing as necessary. An open canoe in such water is best slowed by backpaddling to allow it more time to rise to the larger waves, thus reducing the risk of swamping.

An expert open boat paddler will often run a series of haystacks completely broadside. He can "get away with this" because he has the skill to know when there are no rocks hidden in the haystacks and the skill to return to an aligned position with only one or two strokes.

Setting (Back-ferrying). Immediately ahead of you an obstruction blocks the passage. You must cross over above it and at the same time avoid letting the current carry you down on it. This is a basic problem, and to it you apply a basic technique — *setting*. For this you backpaddle with the boat at an angle to the current. The backward component of your motion opposes the downstream movement of the current, and the lateral component carries you across the stream.

Setting is essentially simple. It may appear complex because you must plan a course which is the combined result of two motions — the backward motion of the boat and the downstream flow of the current. But it should be clear that the boat is a freely floating, not a fixed, object, and that the current cannot exert any force on its side. The only lateral movement is that given by paddling toward the side; without a current your rate of approach to the bank would be the same.

Figure 65. Setting (back-ferrying) used to cross a current above an obstruction.

If a canoe team finds that it cannot set with accuracy for any distance, it should practice paddling backward in still water. The paddlers will discover that they still have the same problems of directional control, but now have the space and time to perfect their technique. An hour or two spent paddling backward can bring handsome rewards on the river.

Although there are variations of style possible in setting, it is important that the two paddlers in a double canoe be in complete agreement on their specific roles. Here is a system used by some canoeists. The stern initiates the maneuver with a pry or back sweep which moves his end of the canoe toward the side to which the set is to be made. The angle of the canoe to the current is roughly 20 to 40° — the stronger the current, the smaller the angle. Both paddlers immediately backpaddle, and both help to hold the canoe at the right angle with appropriate back sweep and, if necessary, draw strokes.

As always when backpaddling, the bow has the primary control of direction and should exercise it well. After crossing upstream of the obstruction, the bow draws the canoe back into alignment with the current and both paddlers resume a forward course. (Here we are assuming that setting is occurring in uniform current. Setting from still water into a current is discussed in the next chapter.)

The single canoeist, in setting, can make good use of a praticed backward J-stroke, and, when necessary, the cross backstroke. He cannot afford the landsman's clumsy style of crossing his paddle by changing hands. The kayaker, with strokes available on both sides, has a lesser problem in learning control in setting. He needs only a practiced backstroke.

Running Backward. Occasionally you may have to run a passage backward, at times because it is the best solution to a problem, but more often as the best means of recovering from some miscalculation. Slalom competitions always include "reverse gates," which must be taken backward. Give yourself plenty of practice with this, beginning with easy passages and working up to the moderately difficult, and then when you are forced to do it you can be nearly as cool about it as about a normal forward drop. When running backward, try to memorize the lay of the river with an occasional glance over one shoulder.

Going Upstream. It is difficult to paddle upstream in a swift current. If it is important to move both up and down the river, consider using a setting pole as discussed at the end of the chapter on solo paddling techniques.

Lining. When a passage cannot be safely run on the paddle, the boat can sometimes be worked through it empty, with the paddlers guiding it from shore with the painters. For example, a quick succession of sharp drops over ledges could be, because of the rock configuration, impossible to take on the paddle, yet easy to line next to shore. When lining a boat, be wary of letting it get broadside to the current, since a pull on the painter can then capsize it quickly. If it does begin to turn, a timely, gentle snubbing on the upstream painter may straighten it out and ward off trouble; if not, try to let it ride down to where the current is weaker or where it can be pulled in a more favorable direction. A long painter is a help here; it is often worthwhile to tie another one to the painter to get a good working length. Use great caution when snubbing with the downstream painter when the boat is in a current, for this can snap it broadside for a quick capsizing.

Tracking. This is the use of the painter to work a boat upstream. In a stong rapid, don't try it; portaging is easier and safer. However, in a mild rapid with a fairly uniform current, you can use bow and stern painters in conjunction to hold the bow slightly farther out in the current than the stern as you work up along the shore. This is something like kite flying on the horizontal. When the shoreline is rough, you can, less elegantly, scramble along and pull from rock to rock. This is usually slow work and feasible only for short distances.

Landing. In a current, always bring the upstream end of the boat to shore first. You can set in, stern first, or bring the bow to an upstream landing after an eddy turn at the shore. Superfluous though it may seem, it is worth a reminder to take the painter ashore with you and tie it or beach your boat securely. Even old hands have been surprised and embarrassed by a runaway boat.

CHOOSING A COURSE

The running of quick water requires picking the most advantageous channels, avoiding obstructions, and dealing with fast currents. To survive all but the easy rapids, you must plan ahead. As you go, constantly shift your attention from the near to the more distant problems so that you will have a prospective course as far as you can see. Be prepared to revise it as you go, but never be without one. An easy channel, chosen casually, can lead you into a cul-de-sac, when a more obscure or less tempting route chosen with foresight would have bypassed it. For some of the more intricate passages a good plan must include not only the *where,* but the *how;* at times your paddle strokes must be as specific and appropriate as a climber's holds.

Whenever you are in any substantial doubt because of an unusually steep patch, a blind corner, a boulder patch, or a fallen tree across the channel, land. Scramble along the bank and look it over carefully. Plan every move, when that is necessary. If after that you are still in doubt, don't run it. Line down if you can, or carry around.

Water flowing downhill in an unobstructed channel, as in a canal or sluiceway, is slowed by friction at the sides and bottom; the fastest flow is in the middle and at the top. This is generally true in rivers, but a complex flow pattern is superimposed on the basic layer arrangement by an array of hydraulic phenomena. The current is deflected by obstructions, narrowed into fast descending chutes and then abruptly slowed, strained through boulder patches, shallowed by descents over broad ledges and shoals from the river's own washings, or driven into sharp turns by the underlying rock formations. The resulting variations of water velocity and direction demand of the boater a skill at reading the water to know in advance how to adapt himself to this pattern of change. A good boater develops the habit of analyzing every flow pattern he sees; what he learns from the shore will supplement his experience on the river.

Picking a channel. In any river, the current velocity is higher with increasing steepness of the gradient, with absence of obstructions, and toward the middle of the stream away from the drag of the river bed. At normal water levels, take the fastest water; this is the river's choice of channel, deeper and less obstructed than the surrounding part, and a good one for the boater as well. In high water this main current can become

93

a turbulent roller coaster. For sheer excitement, ride it — unless you have an open canoe which would swamp in the haystacks, unless the current could carry you beyond the point of safe exit from it, or unless it is in fact too rough for safety. Then the best course is at the edge of the main current, between the lurking rocks and the midstream turbulence.

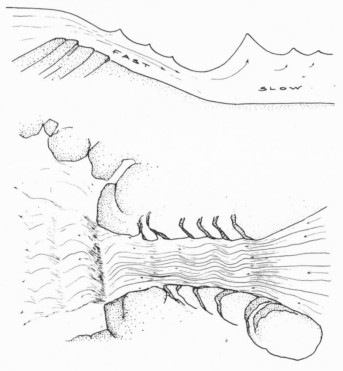

Figure 66.   The formation of standing waves at the bottom of a fast chute.

In rocky streams, it sometimes happens that the best channel is not evident at first sight. As you approach a drop, look for the strongest current. This is the best clue to those channels still ahead and blocked from view which are most open to passage. A channel of slower water may well be obstructed somewhere ahead, and so, very likely, will you. As you approach the first accelerating rush of the drop, the main chute will be marked by a smooth tongue of fast water. Follow it. Even where the water drops over a damlike ledge, a smooth, sinuous quality of the flow will mark the points affording the best passage. Look ahead. The fast runout below a sharp drop will give you a further aiming point; foamy or merely choppy areas indicate a poor passage immediately above.

The smooth tongue of water at the beginning of a chute is formed by accelerating water funneled in at the top. During its descent this water will dissipate some of its energy in standing waves. A regular succession of these indicates good depth. More energy will be given up at the bottom of the drop, and here will be found at least one large standing wave, or usually a series of such waves. Again, these haystacks indicate good depth.

Where the river has washed sand or gravel into shoals, look for the biggest waves as an index to the best depth. You should also find, of course, that the current over these sections is stronger. Smooth or merely ruffled water will testify to the shallows beneath, and a possible grounding.

Where islands divide the river into multiple channels, take the channel which drops soonest, other things being equal. A channel which does not drop will often have an abrupt and therefore obstructed dropping point downstream, and at the same time will lose water in successive installments to its neighboring lower channel. It is thus not to be trusted.

River Bends. On river bends, where there is material which can be washed by the current, whether it be sand or flood-carried boulders, the deeper channel is always on the outside of the bend, with loose material shoaled up on the inside. If you need only find the deepest channel, take the outside.

When the river is high and fast and the bend sharp, it can be a trap. Then the faster surface current is swept by centrifugal force to the outside, where it rolls under at the outer bank; there is often an additional cross-current from water pouring off the rocky inside slope toward the main outside current. These two currents combine to force the boat toward the outer bank into obstructions, or with very high water to trap it against an outside wall, unless you hold a course close to the inside of the bend.

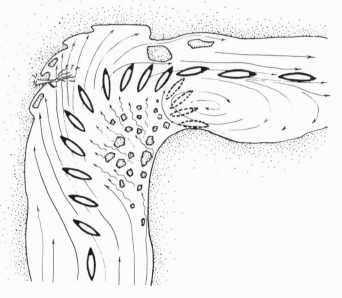

Figure 67.   Setting around a sharp river bend.

This can be done in two ways. For the greatest control use steady backpaddling while holding the stern toward the inside, as in setting. The surface current here is not at all parallel to the banks but is often sharply angled toward the outside, and you must hold the angle of the boat relative to this current, and not to the bank. The alternative method is to head the bow sharply toward the inside of the bend while paddling forward. You may finish off with a turn into the eddy at the inside of the drop. This more dashing style of running a bend allows less time to maneuver and requires a more precise handling of the boat; it is sometimes better suited to the quicker slalom canoes and kayaks than to standard cruising canoes.

Obstructions. Rocks lying just below the surface will hump up the water flowing over them; the form of the hump varies from smooth to abrupt and foamy according to the shape, size, and depth of the rocks and to the speed of the current. Downstream from the rock itself, often at some distance, there will be a standing wave which may be more prominent than the hump over the rock. Do not mistake this wave for the location of the rock. When there is a profusion of subsurface rocks, the surface turbulence can somewhat resemble that of standing waves. The difference lies in the more regular and patterned appearance of standing-wave turbulence in contrast to the jumbled aspect of a submerged rock patch. Most turbulent areas, however, combine standing waves and rocks, and as you look down a long stretch of tumbling water from the head of a drop, your guesses about what lies underneath will become certainties only as you approach each particular patch of water, and this with assurance only after a certain amount of experience.

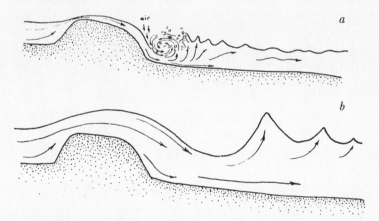

Figure 68.   Flow patterns over a rock with varying water depth. As the depth increases, the foamy eddy behind the rock gives way to the pillow and haystack pattern of (b).

Usually the view of a rapid looking back upstream is much more revealing of the topography of the streambed than the downstream view as you run it, and it is often worthwhile to glance back at a pitch you have just run to relate the downstream water patterns to the upstream topography.

When there are alternate passages among rocks, watch — and feel — where the main current is going. If it tends to carry you into one channel rather than another, go with it unless it carries a penalty. Don't do battle with the current except in an emergency, or you may create one.

When the current is strong and the rocks are coming thick and fast, there will come times when the bow is heading straight toward a rock, despite all your efforts. This is above all the time to keep working. Your desperate last-second draw will be helped by the flow of water around the rock.

Fallen Trees. Fast-moving water is slowed down, piled up, and deflected around an exposed boulder, and the resulting cushion of water helps the paddler to avoid and pass it. But fallen trees make effective traps for the unwary just because they lie across the swift outside current on or near bends — the same current which has undercut and downed them. If you see a tree down ahead, it is a safe bet that the current would carry you into it, and that you must begin evasive tactics well in advance. If you do let yourself be carried into a tree, you risk a very quick and vicious capsize from the pull of the current on the bottom. Holding a branch makes it only more certain. Once in the water, your clothing and life preserver can become snagged, and you may even have to cut yourself free. Thus if there is any doubt about a safe passage, stop well in advance and plan your course, lining or carrying around if necessary. And if some mistake ever does carry you into a tree, try to work through an opening head-on without holding.

VI

Problems in Crossing Currents

In an obstructed rapid some of the flow may be sucked upstream in an eddy, be deflected at right angles by a ledge or boulder, or simply move downstream with a velocity different from that of the neighboring water. These currents are often separated by sharp boundaries; here are some very abrupt velocity changes, and the mark of an expert paddler is skill in handling these boundaries.

Boundary-Line Effects. To use an eddy you must cross its boundary. Consider what happens when the bow is facing upstream in the still water of an eddy and then moves out into fast-moving current. The upstream end of the boat is now in fast water and the downstream end is in the slack water of the eddy. For the unprepared, this crossing has a quick one-two punch. First, the opposing currents grip the ends of the boat and spin it around. Second, the current you are just entering is coming at you from the side and tends to roll the bottom of the boat out from under you. Any current acting broadside to the boat will tend to roll it, and a fast current can flip it almost instantaneously. In turning into an eddy from fast water, the relative lateral movement tends to roll the boat to the downstream side. Similarly, in moving out of an eddy with the bow upstream, the boat tends to roll upstream during the entry into the new current. Unprepared you can upset in even a moderate current. This is just like having a rug pulled out from under you, and every paddler must flip at least once to realize how astonishingly fast it can happen.

It need not happen, however. With good management of boat and paddle, you can use this current differential for turns into and out of eddies. If you want, you can minimize and counteract the twist at the eddy line to cross it without turning. But in every crossing of a current boundary you must oppose the capsizing force by leaning your weight away from the relative oncoming current in combination with an appropriate paddle technique.

Leaning and Bracing. The capsizing force of a strong lateral current is double: first, the sudden sideward acceleration produces the familiar rug pulling effect, and second, the lateral flow of water under the curve of the hull sucks down on the upstream side. You can counter both these forces by leaning away from the oncoming water, tipping the hull to offer the bottom, rather than the bilge, to the current. At the same time, your weight is used as a counterbalance. Here we will review the bracing strokes discussed earlier with particular emphasis on how they apply when entering and leaving eddies. A brace can support a surprising portion of your weight, and thus enable you to use your body effectively as a counterbalance in the most abrupt boundary crossings.

Varieties of Bracing Strokes. In both canoe and kayak the paddle is used to maintain stability. These bracing strokes can be separated into two types: reactive and anticipatory.

A reactive brace is primarily a defensive measure, thrown in quickly to oppose a threatened upset by an unexpected current or a tossing haystack. The stroke is downward, in order to recover to an upright position. It can be a low brace with the nonpower face of the paddle, or a high brace with the power face. The stroke can vary in degree from a slight downward shift of a normal forward stroke to a desperate push to roll you back off your beam ends. Lean your body to the same side so that you first return the boat to a stable position, and then bring yourself back to the vertical. In every case, the distinguishing characteristic of a reactive brace is that it is made on the side toward which you are already tipping.

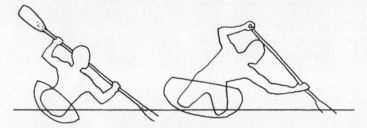

Figure 69. Typical forms of the high brace in the kayak and the canoe.

An anticipatory brace, on the other hand, is made on the side away from the one to which you would otherwise tip, and is combined with a lean to that side. The duffek, or hanging, strokes in both kayak and canoe are anticipatory braces as well as strong turning strokes. These anticipatory braces are at the heart of modern technique in turning and crossing current boundaries. The capsizing force which you encounter in such turning and crossing is opposed by leaning against it in advance; the bracing stroke supports the lean, and this support comes not from a downward stroke but from the force of moving water on the blade. The last phase of an anticipatory brace is that of recovery to the upright, and here you may use a light downward stroke. For all anticipatory bracing strokes, the basic rule is to lean and brace away from the current toward the inside of a turn.

The principle of leaning and bracing applies equally to canoe and to kayak, but the techniques differ to suit the nature of the boats. Because of the open boat's greater inherent stability, its paddler will bend at the waist to lean farther than the boat tips. With the kayak or C-1 it is the reverse; here, the boat's narrow hull allows the paddler to tip it with a hip motion high against an oncoming current while maintaining a body lean no more than that needed for a dynamic balance.

A C-1 paddler will also use a cross high brace when entering fast water, as will the solo boater. Here the stroke is placed well forward by leaning both forward and to the side.

The back brace is also useful for turning, particularly in the kayak. Since this stroke combines the functions of bracing and prying, it is particularly suited to turning downstream when leaving an eddy or turning into a slalom gate. It is thus complementary to the high brace.

All hanging strokes combine the functions of bracing and drawing — they support a lean and pull sideward at the same time. In the double canoe, the control when turning is shared by both paddlers, but the single paddler, in either kayak or canoe, uses one blade for all control. From his centered position in the boat he can apply the sideward force forward, amidships, or astern, or vary his paddle position in the course of a single stroke to modify the turning effect. The high braces provide both stability and control in turns across current boundaries and are indispensable for the repertoire, not just of the expert, but of every paddler.

Which Side for the Canoe Paddle. When moving from still water to fast, it is obvious from the discussion above that there is a considerable advantage in having the bow paddle on the downstream side. Some paddlers will shift paddle sides to accomplish this; however, it is not necessary. A cross high brace is an excellent tandem stroke and should be mastered by any serious bow paddler. While the bow is in the crossed-over position the boat has no upstream brace available. Thus, the cross high brace must be accompanied by a lean out over the water to counteract the tendency of the current to roll the boat upstream.

VII

Eddies and Their Uses

Immediately downstream of almost every obstructing boulder and exposed ledge, in midstream or at the shore, lies an eddy. Here the water flows upstream, then is peeled off by the current shooting past its upper edge. A midstream eddy is roughly symmetrical and has its strongest flow at the midline; an eddy at the river's edge has its strongest back circulation at the bank itself. The fast downstream current and the adjacent eddy water meet at a sharp boundary; it is here that the ability to lean and brace against a countercurrent is most put to use.

Eddies are produced by the very conditions — strong currents and obstructed passages — that make them useful or necessary in running the river. They are small islands of quiet water in the midst of the flood where you can arrest your downstream motion to wait for your companions, stop to assess the water ahead, turn your bow for an upstream crossing, or prepare for a complex maneuver.

Setting into an Eddy. The least abrupt way to enter an eddy is to set into it, stern first. Plan your course to slide closely past the obstruction, backpaddling to cut your speed. At the moment that the stern is clear, use a strong back sweep stroke to put the stern into the top of the eddy. In a double canoe, the bowman helps to check the forward speed with backstrokes during the entry, and both paddlers may need to continue with a few backstrokes immediately afterward to hold the boat at the top of the eddy.

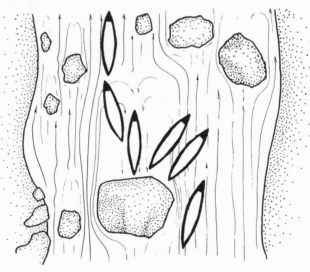

Figure 70.   Setting into an eddy.

In this entry the stern crosses the eddy line first, with the downstream end — the bow — leaving the current last. The current forces the bow to follow the stern into the eddy, and thus forces the boat back into alignment. Use the set for entering an eddy if you are already setting for some other reason. Otherwise, it is faster and more fun to use the eddy turn described below.

Leave the eddy at its weak lower end. You will discover, if you try it, that you cannot paddle forward downstream across a strong eddy line; the pressure of the current on the outside will prevent the bow from leaving the eddy. On the other hand, if you try to set, stern first, across the strong upper end of the boundary, you invite a quick spin and possibly an upset if the current differential is of some strength.

Eddy Turn. Use of the current is the key to a successful eddy turn. Any type of boat does an eddy turn the same way, even though the strokes used to accomplish the turn may vary. The sequence of events for the boat is as follows:

1. The boat slows somewhat and gets at least partly broadside to the main current somewhat upstream of the obstruction causing the eddy.

2. The bow is placed in the still water of the eddy.

3. The main current spins the stern around while the forward momentum brings the boat the rest of the way into the still water.

4. The bow boater leans upstream to counteract the pull-out-the-rug effect of the still water.

For a kayak an eddy turn on either side uses the same sequence of strokes. Start with a sweep stroke on the side away from the turn to bring the bow about and into the eddy just below the obstruction. With careful timing this sweep stroke

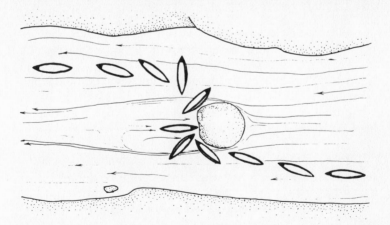

Figure 71. An eddy turn below a midsteam boulder, followed by a turn down-stream into the current on the opposite side.

will move the front of the boat all the way across the eddy line. The following stroke is a duffek used first to complete the turn and second as a high brace so that the boat can be leaned away from the still water.

For the solo canoe or C-1, an eddy turn is more of a challenge since the strokes vary depending on whether it is an on-side or off-side turn. For an on-side turn the change in direction can be initiated by a C-stroke in the forward quarter or by a stern pry far aft. If one is moving faster than the current the change in direction can also be initiated by a duffek straight out to the side. In all cases there must be enough forward momentum to carry the bow into the still water, or an extra forward stroke must be taken. Enter the eddy with a duffek and high brace. If the boat has too much spin you may have to check it with a cross bow forward stroke angled to push water under the bow.

The off-side eddy turn starts with a sweep stroke on the on-side to change the heading and place the bow. Follow with a cross reverse sweep and high cross brace as the boat swings into the eddy. To remove excessive spin use a forward stroke with a large amount of C-stroke at the beginning.

For a tandem canoe an eddy turn starts when the stern-man shifts the boat angle toward broadside. Both paddlers take a forward stroke to place the bow in the still water. The bow plants his blade in the eddy on the upstream side and leans using either a high brace or a cross high brace while the current swings the boat. Both paddlers paddle forward and lean as required.

It is common to see an eddy turn started correctly by a stern pry and then ruined when this stroke is held too long so that it has the effect of a back stroke when a forward stroke is wanted. No back strokes are used in an eddy turn.

It is important to emphasize that it is the boat interacting with the current that is essential in an eddy turn. A good

exercise for tandem paddlers is to see whether the stern paddler can do an eddy turn without any help from the bow. This
excercise requires good timing, but will help the novice to see
how important it is to use the river rather than brute force.

Get the Bow in Early. Whatever the type of boat doing the
eddy turn, it is important to place the bow into the still water as
close to the obstruction as possible. If you never hit the rock in
an eddy turn, you are not trying to enter high enough in the
eddy.

*Figure 72. Turning downstream from an eddy. The canoe is just entering the
current, which is moving down from the right of the picture. The bowman is
leaning and bracing downstream.*

Turning Downstream from an Eddy. The current differential
at the eddy line is as useful in leaving the eddy as it is in
entering it. Lean downstream — that is, away from the oncoming current and toward the inside of the turn. You must paddle
forward (upstream) decisively and at an angle to cross the eddy
line; if you only nose into the current, you will be rotated at the
eddy line without moving through it. The distance of penetra-
tion of the current depends not only on your speed, but also on

the exit angle and the amount which you help or hinder the turning effect of the current by your use of the paddle. The use of the paddle for both turning and bracing is like that for the turn into the eddy.

In solo canoe and kayak there must be enough forward motion to get the bow well out into the fast water. For the kayak or on-side C-1, brace well forward with a duffek. For an off-side turn in the C-1 use a forward cross high brace. In tandem the bow paddler uses a high brace draw on the downstream side while leaning far out over the water.

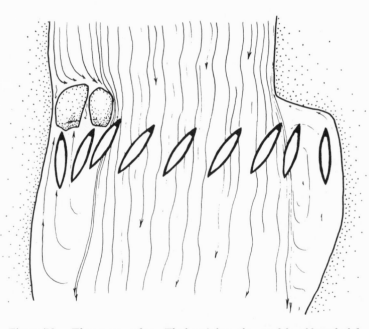

Figure 73. The upstream ferry. The boat is brought out of the eddy at the left with bow upstream, then paddled forward at an angle to cross the current, entering the eddy at the right in this example.

Upstream Ferrying. A canoe or kayak can be driven faster and handled more precisely when paddled forward than it can backward. When you want to cross a fast current without being carried downstream, use the power and control of forward paddling for an upstream ferry, in which you cross by paddling with bow upstream at an angle to the current.

Use an eddy to get into a bow-upstream position. Paddle ahead across the eddy line to place the bow in fast water. The important moment in a ferry occurs just as the bow enters the current. The stern must also enter the fast water almost immediately or a turn will result rather than a ferry. Speed when crossing the eddy line will help, but usually there must also be some force applied near the stern to get it into the fast water.

For a solo canoeist or a kayaker, a draw near the stern on the downstream side will do. It is much more difficult to move the stern when paddling C-1 or tandem stern on the upstream side. The problem here is that only a stern pry is available, but this stroke must be applied in the still water where it is ineffective, while a draw on the opposite side would interact with the fast current. In these cases try to cross the eddy line very fast and almost parallel to it. Many C-1 paddlers simply shift to paddling on the downstream side before doing such a ferry. This is good for those equally skilled on either side.

Once both ends of the boat are in the fast water, merely maintain a convenient angle and the boat will head toward the far shore without going downstream.

Eddy Hopping. A few scattered boulders — and their eddies — in a fast current can make easy work of an upstream ferry. You can use the back current of an eddy to go directly upstream, then out across the current to the next, and so on. With crafty planning, you can paddle surprising distances upstream in fairly strong rapids.

Setting across a Chute. A difficult maneuver that is well worth learning is the set or stern upsteam ferry when it is done across a chute. Here the problem is the same as with the bow upstream ferry. The downstream end must also get into the fast water or the boat will spin around.

109

Learning to Ferry and Set. Practice these maneuvers first in chutes with slow-moving current. Work slowly and deliberately, studying how the current acts on the boat. Then move on to faster chutes. With practice you will find it possible to cross a fast-moving chute with only one or two strokes.

TECHNIQUES FOR PADDLING IN HEAVY WATER

Phenomena of Heavy Water. As the volume of water increases, the severity of the problems it offers can vary enormously. One finds bigger standing waves and rougher turbulence, bigger eddies, and stronger currents with more violent transitions across their boundaries. The paddler is slapped, bounced, and hurried. His lead time for every maneuver is scanty and his indecision can be quickly turned into error. To ride the river safely, he must use its own force to drive, turn, and arrest his passage. For this he must be accurate and decisive in exploiting the eddies and current differentials to the utmost. And he must learn anew to read the water, less to gauge the subsurface obstructions than to predict currents and their effects on his boat.

High water tranforms almost every aspect of a river. Many rocks are submerged and do no more than add to the general turbulence. Big "white eddies" are present. They are formed when a thick sheet of water, pouring over a large obstruction such as a boulder or ledge, plunges deep below, sucking air into the top to make a foamy backflow at the surface. The white eddy has a meager buoyancy and the foamy upper layer gives poor purchase for the paddle. It is made to order for broaching, and because its boundary has both current and buoyancy differentials, it is tricky water.

Haystacks in heavy water can rise to impressive heights, and when they occur as the result of a pair of currents being funneled into a chute from both sides, they take a sharply pyramidal form. It is quite possible to teeter on one of these and be unable to reach with your paddle into the trough at the side. Taken off-center, such a haystack will tend to roll you into the trough, owing to the double effect of the slope and the impinging side current. Counter this by bracing toward the other side.

A long pitch with large standing waves will often have alleys of lesser turbulence where the wave patterns cancel each other. In an open canoe, you may have to seek these out to avoid swamping during a drop.

Maintaining Stability. In running down through turbulence and standing waves in a canoe, keep your paddle in the water for stability, except when you must lift it for a stroke. Like the balancing pole of the high-wire acrobat, it is there when you need help. The blade buried in the water has an enormous potential leverage. Alternatively, you can use a back brace in both canoe and kayak, leaning easily on it as you go. When using forward strokes, lean into them as potential bracing strokes.

The paddler of a single canoe, always vulnerable to upset on the unguarded side opposite his paddle, will lean regularly toward his paddle side for insurance against the effect of unexpected turbulence and cross-currents. He will find it especially useful to keep the paddle in a low brace position during the recovery from a forward stroke.

Paddle Forward in Heavy Water. The boater always has more ability to maneuver when moving faster than the water. It is particularly important not to drift through turbulent water. Even bracing strokes are more effective when moving with respect to the current, but most important is to have enough momentum to climb to the top of a really big standing wave or to punch through an unexpected souse hole with its strong back-curler.

The Open Boat in Big Waves. It is all too easy to bury the bow in a wave and find that the boat is suddenly half full of water. This usually happens when the boat is allowed to drive straight into the wave. The answer is a change of technique. Take really big waves somewhat broadside. This is called *quartering* the wave, since it interacts with the boat on the bow quarter; however, even a partly broadside approach may not be sufficient in heavy water. Many boaters take the big ones completely broadside, and then rotate back to line up with the current before the next obstruction. Finally, if the boat does take on water, don't give up. Brace and keep control. Work to shore, or to an eddy where the water can be rolled out. Those who regularly ride big waves need extra flotation. (See the chapter on equipment.)

Use of Standing Waves. You can take advantage of the large standing wave usually found at the bottom of a chute or an unusually fast drop. Use the upstream face of the wave when you want to oppose downstream motion and the downstream face when you want to accelerate it. Because eddies occur below constrictions through which the water has been accelerated, there is often a large standing wave outside the upper end of such an eddy. If the boat is brought into the eddy on the upstream face of this wave, it will tend to slide off it into the upper end of the eddy, facilitating the turn. The same wave can again be used for the turn downstream out of the eddy. Plan your exit to drive the bow up on the downstream face of this wave. This will help in establishing the lean and turning the bow downstream.

A heavy chute will sometimes produce a particularly large standing wave just below it. If you want to make an upstream ferry here, plan to enter the current so as to ride across on the upstream face of this wave. The boat will tend to coast downhill — but upstream — as in surfing, and you can ferry across to the other side with a minimum of effort, with gravity working for you. Avoid driving the bow down into the trough at the bottom, for then the boat becomes difficult to manage. Riding a standing wave in this fashion takes practice, but it is worth it.

VIII

Coping with River Hazards Safely

RIVER HAZARDS AND WHAT TO DO ABOUT THEM

The first principle of safety is to keep out of trouble. And, since trouble does come, as a rule, in standard packages, it is worthwhile to look at some of them.

Inability to Stop. The hell-for-leather boater or the indecisive one, surprised by a blocked passage or a hazardous drop, may be unable to stop until a midstream boulder does it for him. The prudent paddler keeps a constant eye out for the pools, eddies, and free bits of shore he can use for stopping. Even more, he has cultivated the skill to do it. Precise command of the eddy turn pays off here; there is often no neater or more effective way of getting out of a current in a short distance.

Overturned Boats. If the paddler just ahead gets into trouble, you may be in trouble too. Narrow rivers where there is only one passage are particularly treacherous, especially in low water where one's canoe or kayak can become momentarily hung up and stuck on a hidden rock. Being stuck is usually no problem, but being stuck with another boat just behind is another matter entirely. Proper spacing between boats requires experience and judgment. Too much space and boaters cannot lend assistance to each other when needed. Too little space and they will all pile up each time someone hangs up.

Fallen Tree. This is a most embarrassing variety of upset, because it is usually easily avoided. As we saw earlier, downed trees have usually been undercut by a fast current on the outside of a curve — the very current you are riding as you approach. The situation is dangerous just because it is deceptive. Remedy: get out of the current well upstream. Stop if necessary.

Swamping. During the course of a drop through big waves, an open canoe can pick up a considerable amount of water over the gunwales. Even a small amount of water acts as shifting ballast which impairs stability, buoyancy, and maneuverability. To accept the first stage of disablement is to invite the next and final one. Land and empty at the first chance, lest you be unable to do so later. Do not attempt to bail a canoe with a lot of water in it. Get into shallow water and roll the boat up on its side. If the boat is full, roll it first in the water to get most of the water out, and then roll it on the shore.

Upstream Lean. You are in a tandem canoe, making an upstream exit from an eddy into a current, with the bowman on the downstream side. The bow swings downstream during the entry; the bowman reaches upstream to draw; then the upstream gunwale dips and you are in. Prevention: lean downstream for every entry into a current. The bow paddler should use a high brace or a cross high brace to support the lean.

Broadsiding on a Rock. You are crossing a current upstream of a rock. You miscalculate; the stern is caught in the faster current to the side; the boat turns broadside and is about to fetch up sharply on the rock. This is a perilous moment; the rock will push back high on the side and the current will suck down the upstream gunwale. Act fast. Put your weight on the downstream gunwale to keep the boat upright, or better, to tip it in the opposite direction. Using your paddle, push off the rock and work the boat along until you can turn downstream. With a canoe, sometimes jumping out on a rock or into shallow water is the best way to prevent capsizing and free the boat. Don't hesitate to get your feet wet if by this you can avoid swamping. Never, however, risk being caught in the water downstream of a swamping canoe.

When the bow rather than the middle of the boat hangs up on a rock or other obstruction, the current will tend to swing the stern around. Trying to fight this often leads to capsizing, but if the stern has room to swing completely around, the bow can usually be freed. In an open canoe either both paddlers tandem or one solo can turn around to run the passage with the boat reversed until it can safely be turned again. In a kayak or decked canoe you must also run backward; previous practice in doing this pays off handsomely at this point.

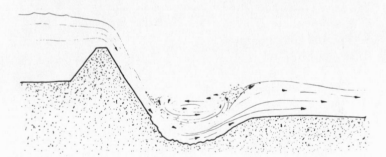

Figure 74. A cross-section of the flow pattern below a dam, showing the formation of the aerated roller and the upward slope of the following back-wave.

Dams, Rollers, and Back-Waves. The danger of weirs or dams — and even low dams can be dangerous — is not in the initial drop from the upper to the lower level, but in the roller and the back-wave which follow it. The falling water plunges over the dam and continues down to the bottom of the river bed, then recurves and returns to the surface some distance downstream. The surface water from this upwelling is partially sucked back to the base of the fall, forming the roller. This roller is aerated and foamy, and gives little support for the boat or purchase for the paddle. A boat caught here will be sucked back under the fall, to remain trapped by the return current, rolling over and over. So will a person. Compounding the danger, just downstream of the roller the surfacing current rises in a back-wave — an uphill surface which can be difficult or even impossible to climb. This sharply raised level of the current is called a hydraulic jump, and it marks the transition stage in which the kinetic energy from the fall becomes potential energy of height.

You can sometimes watch a log caught under such a fall. It will roll over and over at the base of the fall, at times being sucked under only to shoot back up where the current emerges and be carried back to begin the cycle again. A dam as low as three or four feet with a sufficient volume of water running over it can have a fully formed roller trap. Such dams have more than once been fatal to canoeists. Do not attempt to run a dam when there is even a small chance of being trapped. Self-rescue may be impossible, and rescue by others may be difficult or too late.

If, through failure to plan, you have no alternative to running a potentially dangerous dam, be sure to run it straight, for broaching will immediately trap you in the roller: paddle to keep up speed as you drop over, then drive forward when you reach the lower water. This is where you can be deceived into believing that you have safely made it. Not yet, for you must still drive out of the roller and back-wave trap. Plunge the paddle deep to get a grip on the forward-moving water at the bottom; the surface is not only moving against you, but may be so full of air that it offers little purchase.

If you swamp and must leave your boat, your best chance of swimming is sometimes to dive with the main current at the base of the dam, letting it help you get under the back-current of the roller. In one mishap under a low dam, the swamped canoe in its gyrations became aligned with the current, and the paddler was able to pull himself hand-over-hand down the canoe to escape the roller and swim downstream to safety. He was lucky.

Ledges and Souse Holes. A ledge in a river is, in effect, a short, low dam and can produce the same kind of roller and back-wave as a dam. Just below the ledge is usually a powerful eddy, aerated from the falling water. This white eddy, or souse hole, can be an effective and sometimes dangerous trap if the boat is allowed to get broadside. The back-current at the surface and the water pouring in at the top of the eddy combine to pull the boat broadside and then capsize it. When running a ledge, pick the point of strongest flow over it. This can be distinguished by the thicker water at the lip and the faster runout below the ledge. Run it straight to avoid broaching. In heavy water a fully developed white eddy can stop you dead. Use deep strokes into the bottom current to drive forward out of it, and if you should begin to turn broadside, use a deep paddle brace downstream to pull yourself out with the bottom current.

EQUIPMENT HAZARDS

Lost Paddles. A few years ago a double canoe was halfway down a twisting drop. The stern broke his paddle, and in the excitement the bow lost his. The spare was tied in so well that the two paddlers could only ride helplessly to an inescapable conclusion. Keep your spare handy and available. Use thin, easily broken cotton twine for holding such items.

Floating Boats. The more submerged a swamped boat is, the more difficult it is to rescue; and most canoes and kayaks sink right up to their gunwales. The use of additional flotation material can make self-rescue far easier. Polyethylene foam, styrofoam, or even inner tubes securely fastened can make the difference, as discussed in the chapter on equipment.

A decked canoe or kayak which has upset in heavy water will usually float high upside down. Leave it that way. Trying to

117

right it before bringing it to safety will fill it and give the river a grip it did not have before.

Getting Tangled in the Equipment. Keep a mental checklist to prevent being entangled or caught in case of an upset. These things could all cause trouble — a long, loose painter casually thrown into the canoe; a loose spray skirt which could wrap around your legs in the water; a fabric deck not positively attached to the canoe. The low bow seat of the aluminum canoe is a special case of a foot catcher, particularly if you wear heavy boots. Kneel with your heels pointing out to give clearance for a quick exit. The best precaution is to remove the seat and substitute a simple thwart.

Painters. These can be crucial in the rescue of boats, particularly the fish-slippery fiberglass decked canoe or kayak. One means of fastening the free length of painter is a deck loop of shock cord. A grab loop at each end of a kayak can be substituted for the painter, but it is of lesser value in rescue.

Swimming. In a current swimming is done on the back with the feet near the surface. Backstroke upstream at an angle which will get you to the most convenient shore or eddy. Never stand in current. A boater with a caught foot can be held under by the current even in very shallow water. The author knows of a case where an experienced boater drowned in only one and a half feet of water due to a caught foot. Hundreds of boaters were watching but were unable to help.

Self-Rescue. On swamping or capsizing, hold on to the paddle and go immediately to the upstream end of the boat. There is nearly a ton of water contained in a standard canoe, and you dare not risk being caught between this moving mass and a downstream rock.

If there are dangerous rapids immediately below, or if the water is very cold and you are not protected against it, you may have to abandon your boat for your own safety. If so, do it immediately. Even the strongest swimmer can do little in a severe rapid and will get dunked repeatedly even while wearing a lifevest. When running difficult rapids in warm weather, wear enough clothing so that, if upset, you will not get abrasions from sliding on rough rocks.

If your own safety does not compel you to abandon your boat, stay with it, always at its upstream end, and work it gradually toward shore. Try to keep it aligned with the current; this will help prevent it from being wrapped around a rock. It is often feasible to swim with the free end of the painter toward shore or some shallow place. Having once gained a secure foothold out of the current, you can then snub the downstream movement of the boat and work it toward shore or the safety of an eddy. You can sometimes succeed in emptying a boat on a midstream rock. If so, empty toward downstream, lest the current catch the lower gunwale and reclaim the boat.

Rescue from Another Canoe. There is usually neither time nor opportunity for rescue in a strong rapid, where handling one's own boat is a task in itself. Most rivers alternate rapid descents and somewhat slower sections, and it is in these slower sections that one can try to pick up a swimmer or catch a boat. In general, always rescue swimmers, especially those without wetsuits, before going after equipment. It is best if the rescue boat has stationed itself beforehand in the most favorable spot. Approach the swamped boat in position to ferry with it; and, holding or snubbing — but not tying — the upstream painter of the swamped boat, work toward the better bank. In fast water the swamped boat can drag you into trouble; be prepared to let go if necessary and try again.

Emptying One Canoe from Another. In a still pool between rapids it is easy to empty another canoe. One paddler stands and grabs a painter from the swamped boat. Lifting on the painter will spill the water out the opposite end of the swamped boat. When most of the water is out, the boat can be turned upside down on the rescue boat or it can be put back in the water almost empty and paddled ashore for a final emptying of water.

Throw Ropes. In hazardous passages, boats may run singly with other boaters stationed on shore with throw ropes. The person with a rope should take a position so that the recovery path of a rescued boater will be through the easiest route to shore. He should also assure himself that he can provide a secure belay for the rescued person. If his line will be used to pull in a boat, he should have it tied in at the bank or be able to snub it around a tree. One man cannot hold a swamped boat against a strong current nor, often, can two.

It is impractical to throw an unorganized rope. The best rescue rope lives in a throw bag, as described in the chapter on equipment. If a second rescue must be done before the bag is restuffed, prepare the rope for throwing by carefully arranging a dozen coils whose diameter is about a foot and a half. Hold the first six coils in the right hand and the second six in the left. Leave some loosely coiled line by your left foot. Throw with a long underhand motion, simultaneously with both hands. Be sure to hold the free end of the rope with a hand or place a foot on it.

Marooned Boaters. Paddlers without boats are sometimes perched upon rocks. If his rock forms a good eddy, you can take the paddler off with a canoe. Never approach a rock from above, but ferry into its eddy or drop below it with an eddy turn.

If canoe rescue is impossible, throw a line with a bowline on the end. The rescuer can use a standing or sitting belay against the pull of the current, allowing the rescued person to swim or wade to shore at the end of the line. No one going into the water on a line should be tied in any way, for a fast current could drag him below the surface. He should hold the loop for instant release, then if necessary swim down the rapid for a self-rescue below.

SALVAGING A BOAT PINNED ON A ROCK

When a boat is not immediately rescued, its most probable fate is a broadside meeting with a rock — often the one on which it originally capsized, although at times a good distance downstream. The current will have inevitably sucked down the upstream gunwale and jammed the bottom against the rock. In a slow current the damage will be light, but the tremendous force of a strong current — four tons on a canoe in a ten-mile-an-hour current — will break up fiberglass and wrap an aluminum canoe right around the rock.

To take a swamped boat off a rock is a subtle job as well as hard work. Once a boat is well lodged on the rocks a minute or two makes little difference. Take time to plan the rescue. In general, avoid using a rope if wetsuited boaters can do it alone, and avoid using a winch if a few people pulling would work. Personal safety is paramount. Do not put people at risk. If a boat cannot be rescued safely, abandon it or come back when the water is lower. Here are a few useful principles for boat rescue.

1. Raising one end will lighten the boat and cut down the pull of the current.
2. Rolling the boat a quarter turn will offer only a side to the current instead of the entire top.
3. Except in the rare case of a perfectly symmetrical position, the current will favor swinging one end downstream. Work with it.
4. If any force is to be applied by a line, do not tie it to painters, thwarts, or seats. They are too easily torn out. Arrange your line to pull on the entire hull.
5. Attach a line to the end of the boat which will be upstream when it has been freed. This line will be useful in getting the boat to shore.
6. In shallow water with a moderate current, several persons may be able to wade out and lift, roll, or turn the canoe to free it. Do not wade in a strong current.
7. Use heavy poles to apply leverage to the hull to raise or turn the boat at one end.
8. A hand winch, anchored to a tree or rock on shore, can be used to pull in the most appropriate direction. The line from the winch may be led over the high side

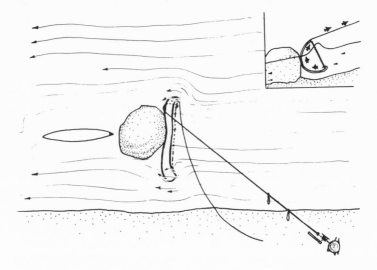

Figure 75.   A typical arrangement of winch and lines for hauling a swamped canoe from a midstream boulder. Butterfly loops are tied into the line beforehand to provide for resetting the winch cable. Not shown is the continuation of the hauling line, which is snubbed around a tree during each repositioning of the winch cable.

of the boat with one turn around the hull and then be fastened to a thwart. This arrangement distributes the load around the entire hull and pulls from the top. The canoe will roll upstream as it starts to come off the rock, making the work easier. In some cases, a simple loop around the hull may be what is necessary. Anchor the end of the rope that formed the loop to a thwart or seat to keep it from sliding off, but make sure that the main pull of the winch is on the hull.

9.   Do not use a rope with much stretch when pulling with a winch. First, you will use up the entire takeup travel of the winch in stretching the line and leave none to move the boat. Second, the stored energy of the stretched line could lash dangerously in the event of a break, either of the line or of one of its fastenings. Nylon is relatively useless with a winch. Manila, da-

cron, and some other synthetics are good. For club use 7/16-inch braided dacron yacht braid is recommended. Samson Paralay brand is good. This line is, however, very expensive.

10. The line on the winch, arranged for best pull in getting the boat off the rock, will be awkward for pulling to shore afterward. Use a line to the bow or stern for this.

11. It is often necessary for the winch to pull for a greater distance than its takeup length. Tie several butterfly nooses in the hauling line, so that, after the first winching, the hauling line can be secured to a tree or rock and the winch cable repositioned to the next loop in the line. See the appendix on knots. Avoid putting any knot in expensive line that cannot be untied.

12. When using a winch, study the situation carefully to see whether several people in the water will be able to safely help with the rescue. Often those in the water can lift at the crucial instant, whereas the rope can only apply force horizontally.

IX

Organizing for Safety and Enjoyment

Organize for Support. Even the most skilled boater will at some time find himself in a situation he cannot handle alone. Often a kayak or C-1 will end up lodged amongst the rocks broadside to the current with no possibility of release by either "unching" the body or pushing with the paddle. Popping the spray skirt might free the paddler but at the sacrifice of the boat. The solution to this problem is simple — mutual support. The scenario described usually occurs on a relatively shallow river where other boaters can come to the rescue, if they are there when needed.

How Many Boats Is Safe? Three boats is the minimum group that can offer good mutual support. Often the nature of the river or the season will dictate that even more strength is desirable. In situations where there is a high probability of injury, the question must not be 'can I get safely off the river?,' but 'can I get an injured boater safely out to transportation?' Three boats is not enough strength for a trip miles from the nearest road or for a trip with boaters of marginal skill for the challenge at hand.

THREE WAYS TO ORGANIZE ON THE RIVER

Single File Organization. The strength of a party and the number of boaters in it will determine the best way to organize. The simplest river formation is running single file. A boater who knows the river is selected as the lead boat, while a second experienced boater *sweeps* or runs last. The sweep usually carries trip safety equipment such as first aid supplies and a winch and ropes if required. The lead boat carries a throw bag, and others may as well. In a long single file the most skilled rescue boat is best placed near the middle of the party. The rules for running single file are:

1. The lead boat is never passed.
2. The sweep never passes any boat.
3. Each boat keeps the one behind it in sight, waiting if necessary.

Single file organization works well with up to seven boats on easy water but is unwieldly on difficult rivers or with more boats. In either of these cases every boat must waste time waiting for the last boat at a large number of drops. In cold weather the very act of waiting can be a hazard, as the entire party becomes chilled.

Independent River Groups. This system depends upon each member of a small river group to continuously know the whereabouts of every other boat. No one can keep track of more than four other boats, and three is better. Thus a natural group is three, four, or five boats, with four being ideal. Running order is not important in a small group, although one may still assign a lead and sweep. All major obstacles are scouted by the whole group and the individuals support each other through the drop by taking up throw rope positions or by standing by as chase boat as required.

Semi-Independent River Groups. A large trip can be safely broken up into a number of four-boat groups, each with its own group leader; but, a few words are in order about how these groups interact. There is still a need for a person familiar with the river in the lead position. He is usually the leader of the lead group. He is responsible for informing his group about important obstacles, portages, dams, etc. The lead group waits at each important feature until this information is properly passed on to the second group, which in turn waits for the third and so on.

A sweep group with extra safety equipment is also useful. On very large trips additional safety gear can be placed near the center of the trip. If throw lines are in order, then there should be a throw line in each group.

Group running order may be fixed by the trip leader, or he may permit groups to pass or be passed — except the lead and sweep. Passing through saves a great deal of time. When a member of one group has a minor problem that requires no attention from the rest of the trip, the following group merely keeps going.

Large trips can be organized around river groups for shuttling of cars and cooking. The Appalachian Mountain Club has run trips for as many as forty-eight boats this way without the river seeming overcrowded. Indeed, forty boats organized into groups can seem like a lot less trouble than ten boats strung out in a row and waiting at every drop.

Getting around Major Obstacles. Even easy trips can have major hazards, such as a newly uprooted tree in the middle of a difficult passage. The most important requirement is to recognize the hazard. It is always safer to run a river with someone who knows it; otherwise, relatively easy looking pitches must be treated as difficult. Here are a few considerations that must be addressed about any major obstacle.

1. Does anyone in the party know this pitch well? Even "horrendous" waterfalls may be runnable by people who have scouted them in low water and found the safe passages.

2. Scout any drop that is both difficult and unknown.

Consider portaging major obstacles when the party is weak or a river is being run for the first time.

3. If the drop is runable, should the lead boat have support from the bank? If so, which points are best for a potential rescue with a throwing rope?

4. Could one boat hang up in a crucial passage so that a following boat would ram it? If so, each boat should wait until that part of the drop is clear.

5. As each boat finishes the drop, should it hold a strategic position there for potential rescue? If so, then it should wait until relieved by a following boat.

Role of the Trip Leader on the River. A large group should always have a leader, and even individual river groups should have someone designated as "being in charge."

Certain responsibilities belong to the leader of a trip or group. He should assure himself that all equipment is in good condition and that rescue gear appropriate to the trip is on hand. He may prescribe procedures for any particularly hazardous drop. He also has the burden of deciding who shall go on the river. He should know the capabilities of each paddler in advance, and if the run is unexpectedly difficult, he may ask some of the less experienced not to run, or he may cancel the run or move the group to some other river. With an uneven group, he may choose to let only the experts run a difficult passage and require the others to go on foot to the bottom of the drop.

Role of the Individual. It is a good rule that the leader can tell you what you should not do, but only you yourself can decide what is safe. If you are feeling poorly but have managed to get on the river anyway, be sure that the leader and the other boaters know that your condition has deteriorated. Sickness and hypothermia are much easier to deal with if they are recognized early. If you are not up to running a difficult drop, line or carry it while the rest of the party is looking it over.

Leading Large River Trips. Little organization is required when three or four friends go off to run a favorite stream. As soon as a group gets so large that people are less well known to each other or the river becomes less well known, some form of trip organization is required.

The Appalachian Mountain Club has led large river trips for many years and has developed a body of leadership lore that is passed on from generation to generation in leadership manuals, training sessions, and so forth. Included in this chapter is a Canoe Leader's Checklist put together by the Club's Interchapter Canoe Committee in 1979. It probably contains more items than most people will need to consider, but it will help the novice leader work out a personal leader checklist.

Who Is the Checklist For? The checklist was written for leaders of club trips. Here "club" means an organization with hundreds of boaters, many of whom do not know each other. It means an organization that publishes trips in a bulletin ahead of time, and it means a group with a formal system for teaching white water boating and rating paddling and leadership skills. The club's leaders have access to both commercially published river guides and privately compiled river folders. The club also has boats that can be rented to its members. There are obviously items on the checklist that less formal organizations can freely ignore.

Planning Ahead. Most "horror stories" occur when the "wrong" group of people starts down a river together. There is no substitute for skill, and an enjoyable trip matches the skills of the boaters to the challenge of the river ahead of time. Turning someone away at the river bank is a major social problem. It is much better to turn the weak paddler back over the telephone. A good leader should learn to "rate" people over the phone. The checklist suggests the right kind of questions to ask. It is not enough to know what rivers someone has been on. The boater who made it down "el supremo" by hook or crook may be inexperienced nonetheless. Ask specific skill questions; they will tell you who you want to share the river with.

Safety Information. Read the Safety Code of the American Whitewater Affiliation in the appendix. This code is the basic safety information that every boater should know. If the group you are leading has no formal program of instruction where this safety information is passed along, consider ordering a supply of safety codes to hand out to new boaters. The ordering address is given in the appendix.

COMMENTS ON THE CANOE LEADER'S CHECKLIST

Who the Checklist Is Written For. This list was prepared to assist trip leaders of the Appalachian Mountain Club. It will thus be most helpful where large groups of people must be dealt with. It does not address the problems of expedition trips, which are away from all help for long periods. Small groups will also find it helpful, though. They need only ignore the information that does not apply. Some of the problems addressed are the need to publish a schedule of trips led by many different leaders, the need to cope with people who may not be personally known to the leader, and the need to organize large groups of people for mutual support while keeping them out of each other's way.

Dealing with Many People. Large trips can test the sanity of even the strong of heart, but they can be made easier to organize if a few principles are followed. First, never promise to do anything for the registrants. Keep the "ball in their court" at all times. Let other people make the extra phone calls or call you later. Make sure your own family members do not promise that you will call back. Get someone else to do every job that can possibly be assigned to another.

Extra People and Equipment. On large or small trips plan a little redundancy. Try to have extras of the crucial items like paddles, lifejackets, and kayak skirts. Two or three small stoves are better than one large one that may fail, for instance.

Coverage is also important when it comes to people. Never leave yourself in a position where a single dropout would compromise the safety of a trip. Most horror story trips were set up to fail during the registration phase. It is particularly easy to set up a failure on a small trip arranged among friends, where there may be considerable pressure to take along an extra friend that the rest of the trip is not strong enough to support.

Responsibility of the Leader. Unless you are a professional guide, you should keep yourself in the role of one who organizes a trip of persons, all of whom assume responsibility for themselves. Establish early on that the leader may prevent the trip members from acts considered unsafe, but that only the individual can decide what he or she can run safely.

Paddler Rating System. Clubs large enough so that not all paddlers know each other's skills firsthand need rating systems. Such systems work best where they are combined with formal instruction. After instruction one can assume certain basic knowledge has been instilled. Even if every skill is not present in a particular paddler, at least the leader can be sure that the paddler has some knowledge of the risk, challenge, and skill requirements associated with a particular class of water. A rating system used by the Appalachian Mountain Club is included here. It is "operational" in that it tries to describe what a person is able to do, while being general enough so that it does not list every stroke and maneuver.

This rating system emphasizes safety and rescue skills. It encourages kayakers to learn how to cope with a swamped open boat and open boaters to master the safe rescue of swimmers.

131

Classification of Rivers. The American Whitewater Affiliation river classification is given in the appendix. It tells how to classify a particular stretch of water. It does not help with unknown rivers. For new rivers there is no substitute for guidebooks and scouting. Leaders will have to do local research to locate guidebooks. In many cases they can scout a planned trip by auto prior to the run.

Club river folders are recommended wherever people operate in organized groups. They list put-ins, take-outs, campsites, river hazards, gauge locations, and other vital information. They can supplement guidebooks or become the beginning of a new book.

Being a Good Neighbor. Increasingly rivers don't just exist, they — or at least their banks — are owned and regulated by individuals or government agencies. Find out who to contact before using put-ins and take-outs and before camping or picnicking. Thank people for their forebearance of our sport and especially write or phone thanks when a government agency or power company gives the boating community a water release.

Figure 76.   Appalachian Mountain Club — Canoe Leader's Checklist

CANOE LEADER'S CHECKLIST

PRIOR TO REGISTRATION — AT LEAST TWO WEEKS BEFORE TRIP

Select river, and choose alternate river to be used if necessary. Review up-to-date information on river. Read river folder or guidebooks.

Obtain permits or permission for parking, camping, fires, crossing private property, etc. Plan for campsite, drinking water, and toilet facilities. Notify state police if traffic considerations will warrant. Ask them if anyone else should be notified.

Notify person in charge of equipment. How many boats may you use? Reserve boats and safety equipment.

Recruit people with skills or equipment needed on your trip (e.g. first aid, rescue and safety, food buying, cooking, river leading, instructing). Consider your own experience, the probable strength of the group, and how you may need to supplement it.

Be sure your own personal equipment is ready.

Plan a menu suitable for the worst weather you may have and the probable crowd.

Prepare registration checklist and form. Decide maximum registration you will accept.

REGISTRATION TIME

Note 1 — Keep a running count of paddlers, and boat space. No more space — have them call you back. Use a form to organize this.
Note 2 — The (*) items below are information you give to applicants either by phone or by mailing a dope sheet.
Note 3 — Newcomers can be good paddlers, but not know local customs. Explain everything.

Who is registering? One person or several?
    Name. Address (if not on club roster). Phone(s). Age (over or under 18). Club member(s). Medical problems — you want to know, but they are responsible.

When? Which day or days? Which meals?

Qualifications. River rating. See below to evaluate newcomer.

    Recent paddling experience and rivers run. Have they had instruction? Skills — ask specific skill questions. Have respondent describe eddy turn, draw, pry, cross draw, ferry, set, etc.

Get name of reference you can call. If you are in doubt, tell them you'll call them back after you've registered the rest of the trip. Then call someone more experienced to discuss and evaluate.

Boat and partner questions.

Is a partner needed? Solo? Willing to do either?

*What boat(s) will they use? If personal, what flotation? If rental, when and where is it to be picked up? If they have a new boat, discuss how it is outfitted.

*If you need space in boat they will bring, be sure they know it. Have an experienced renter sign out boats and safety gear.

No more boat space? Make freeloaders call you back.

Transportation for people and boats.

Car? How many canoes and people can it carry?

*No car? Give out names, phones for possible rides. Make them responsible. (It helps to plan river groups, if you know who will come with whom.)

*Where to go and when; be specific. River(s) and alternate. Meeting time, place, and route to. Second day meeting. Campsite.

Meals and equipment — meals leader will supply. Meals (lunches) and utensils they will bring. Need tent? Special equipment for them to bring, e.g., stove, table, lantern, tarp, ropes and winch, first aid kit, water, trash bags, cook kit or utensils.

*Fees — estimate cost of parking, camping, meals, rentals, etc.

*Cancellations — if trip is dropped, how will word be given? If paddler must drop, whom to phone — number, day, time. Deposit required or fee to be charged late dropout.

WEEK OF THE TRIP

Make final river selection. Scout the river if necessary. Contact recent river leaders or paddlers for information about the river. Know how long run will take. Is there time to accommodate an emergency boat rescue? What is gauge reading? What does it mean?

Make final count of people and boats. Would one dropout ruin things? Do you have extra boat space?

Confirmation of club canoes needed — and safety equipment. Arrange for one person to supervise checkout of rental boats if required.

Preliminary river planning — plan number of groups. Lead paddler, lead group, group leaders, sweep paddler, sweep group. Be sure groups are balanced and self-sufficient. Final decision is made on the river bank. Consider pre-arranging the shuttle. Will you shuttle by groups?

Finalize menu. Purchase food. Rebag or box food by meals — predinner snack, dinner, breakfast. Keep track of expenses.

CHECK-IN TIME AND PRE-RIVER ANNOUNCEMENTS

Be at the meeting place one-half hour early to do check-in. Confirm partners and river groups. Change as needed. Avoid putting one carload into several groups.

Explain your river running rules. For instance:

Single file — stay behind lead, ahead of sweep, keep boat behind in sight.

Groups — Stay behind lead group, ahead of sweep group. State if groups may pass each other and whether each group must keep group behind in sight.

Place people into structure above. Announce lead, sweep, group leaders, location of safety gear. Tell all paddlers that on the river, the river group leader is in charge. Have group leaders discuss internal organization. Get "support" of other experienced boaters for "unpopular decisions."

Discuss river, hazards, take-out, and prearranged dropout point and who to tell if dropping out.

Specify lunch plans. Announce lunch site or time or have lunches kept in cars until after A.M. run.

Remind paddlers to tell someone in their group if they're not feeling up to par. Take note of paddlers' attitudes and health conditions.

Set up shuttle. Explain — if by groups, who is lead car, that one keeps car behind in sight, and whether a car is to be left at the halfway point.

Announce shuttle time. Check lifejackets and safety gear before shuttle leaves.

Place rescue gear, first aid kit, extra clothes, and spare paddles.

Get dinner people on river early.

On the river follow rules set up ahead of time. Scout and even line or portage difficult drops.

Watch self and others for signs of hunger, cold, and fatigue.

Take out at a safe time.

AFTER FIRST DAY'S RUN

Assign meal cooking and chores to individuals or river groups. Post menus or explain menu to head cook. Avoid being your own cook.

Announce when you want breakfast, when to leave camp.

Collect trip fees. Break camp and leave it clean.

Arrange for check-in of club equipment.

Write up trip reports within a week.

Figure 77. Appalachian Mountain Club — Responsibility of the Leader.
In the lists of skill requirements below, each higher classification assumes the paddler to have all the skills listed in the lower classifications.

SKILL REQUIREMENTS FOR OPEN CANOE RATINGS:

Class I - Beginner. Knows basic white water maneuvering strokes. Can handle canoe competently on both sides, bow and stern, in current. Can paddle a canoe with a partner in a straight line without changing sides, can move the canoe sideways, and can rotate the canoe in a circle.

Class II - Novice. Can pick out and negotiate a general route through a simple rapid and can assess immediate obstacles. Can stop forward motion of canoe in current and can set (back-ferry) left and right with a partner. Can do simple eddy turns and ferry maneuvers. Knows river procedures and basic safety principles, including self-rescue.

Class III - Intermediate. Can pick out and negotiate a course through continuous rapids, and can handle isolated stretches

---

of heavy water. Can use bow upstream techniques effectively (eddy turns, ferrying, running backwards). Can do all of the above bow, stern, and single. Can handle canoe with less competent partner in Class II water. Knows and applies principles of scouting, lining, placing of safety boats and line throwers, and rescuing others.

Class IV - Expert. Can maneuver expertly solo in continuous heavy water through drops. Can stop or render assistance to others even in difficult rapids. Skills are second nature. Is fully competent in applying safety and rescue techniques applicable to all classes of boats.

SKILL REQUIREMENTS FOR CLOSED BOAT RATINGS:

Class IK and IC-1 - Beginner. Is stable in the boat and knows how to escape if the boat is caught or overturned. Knows basic maneuvering strokes and can handle the boat competently in swift water. Can paddle in a straight line, back paddle, and turn both left and right. Can move boat sideways.

Class IIK and IIC-1 - Novice. Can pick out and negotiate a general route through a simple rapid and can assess immediate obstacles. Can stop forward motion in a current and set (back-ferry) right and left. Can do simple eddy turns and ferry maneuvers. Knows river procedures and basic safety principles, including self-rescue.

Class IIIK and IIIC-1 - Intermediate. Can pick out and negotiate a course through continuous rapids, and can handle isolated stretches of heavy water. Can do eddy turns, ferry, and run backwards skillfully in current. Has effective command of high and low braces and the duffek stroke. Has done at least one emergency roll in current. Knows and applies principles of scouting, placing of safety boats and line throwers, and the rescuing of others.

Class IVK and IVC-1 - Expert. Can maneuver expertly through continuous heavy water through drops. Can stop or render assistance to others even in difficult rapids. Has a reliable roll and rolls regularly in Class 4 current. Skills are second nature. Can use own boat to push or tow a stricken boat. Is fully competent in applying safety and rescue techniques applicable to all classes of boats.

GROUP SAFETY EQUIPMENT

A group cannot be safe if the individuals are not safely equipped. Each boater needs a lifevest, paddle, helmet, wetsuit, boat flotation, grab loops and painters, and so forth. If the trip is away from the road for any distance or time, a personal first aid kit, food, and extra clothing are also appropriate. These items are further discussed in the chapter on equipment.

Easy Trips. When the group is close to a road and help, a relatively simple first aid kit, spare paddles, and a throw rope may be enough spare equipment.

Ropes for Salvaging Boats. Whenever there is a good chance that spilled boats can become lodged amongst the rocks, a winch line and winch are in order as described in the last section of the chapter on river hazards. A recommended set consists of two twenty-five-foot lengths and one hundred-foot length of seven-sixteenths-inch diameter Dacron Yacht Braid and a ratchet-operated come-along rated at one to two tons. When the river is next to the highway, this gear is often left in the car of someone who is following the group down the run. Always carry duct tape for minor patching of boats after they are damaged.

Trips Away from Help. Whenever the river moves away from help, additional care must be taken. Safety equipment must be located near the rear so no one can be left unprotected. There must be sturdy spare paddles for both canoes and kayaks. The first aid kit should be better and should be carried in a fifty calibre ammunition box or other waterproof container.

Can You Get an Injury Out? Always ask whether you have enough equipment to rescue a severely injured paddler. When away from the road in cold weather, a synthetic fiber-filled sleeping bag and extra clothing are needed. A wetsuit will not keep an inactive person warm. Also, consider a small stove. And, of course, carry matches and fire starting gear. You need enough food and warmth to sustain the victim and at least one person to stay with him or you are not prepared for severe injury. Remember that the most common severe injury in boating is a dislocated shoulder. It is not possible to paddle afterward, even if the shoulder is relocated.

X

*Equipment Selection, Modification and Repair**

PERSONAL EQUIPMENT

Prevention of Hypothermia. For a boater cold is not just uncomfortable, it can easily prove fatal. More people have died from the cold on icy rivers than have actually drowned. The newspaper report calls it drowning, but the drowning occurred because swimming is not possible in ice-cold water without protection.

Clothing — the Old Way to Keep Warm. Conventional clothing is comfortable when dry, but miserable when wet. Canoeists must be prepared to be wet. Dress, therefore, in clothing that retains warmth when wet. Wool and wool-like synthetics retain their loft when wet, and the water drains out immediately, to be replaced with air that insulates even though the fabric is wet. Wool is a fairly good insulator when in the water. The worst fabric when wet is cotton. Avoid it. For rapids cover wool clothing with waterproof pants and parka. Do not use a poncho or raincoat, which will impede swimming. Conventional clothing requires an extra change in a dry pack, which is a nuisance.

Figure 78. Various styles of wetsuits good for boating. Left to right: Farmer John (wear a paddling jacket over it), Shorty (strictly for warm weather but cold water), separate top, full wetsuit (two-piece pants plus top), top worn over a Farmer John (very flexible arrangement, use the top only when cold).

Wetsuits. The only complete protection is given by a diver's wetsuit of neoprene sponge rubber (figure 78). The use of wetsuits is increasingly common among those who run the rivers in the early part of the season. You can be dunked while wearing one and remain comfortable, and you need carry no spare clothing for river bank changes. The heaviest available wetsuits are of quarter-inch material; these are too hot and cumbersome for paddling. The medium thickness of three-sixteenths of an inch is comfortable on a chilly day and makes an icy swim seem almost pleasant. For warmer weather, when the water temperature is nevertheless still low, a suit or jacket of one-eighth-inch material gives enough protection in the water with minimum discomfort out of it. For extremely cold weather add an extra wetsuit vest for more protection over the trunk while the arms are left relatively free. A wetsuit helmet is also a useful addition for Eskimo rolling in ice water.

a

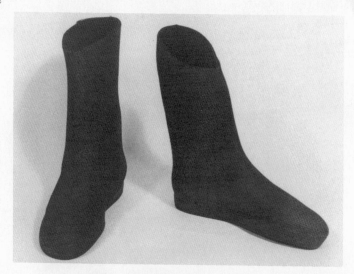

b

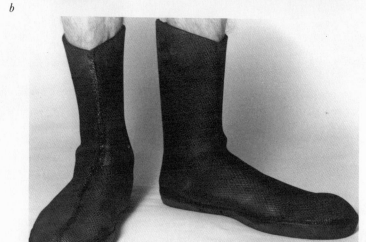

Figure 79. The booties in (a) are thin and must be worn inside oversize sneakers or sandals while those in (b) are heavier and have built-in soles. Booties with double soles are good for scouting and general out-of-the-boat work.

Hand Protection. In moderately cold weather the hands will stay warm if the boater keeps the rest of the body warm. Pay particular attention to the head, which loses heat fast if not covered.

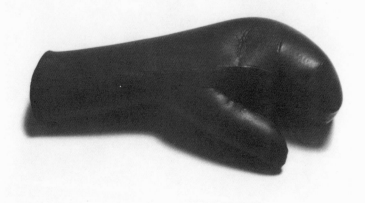

Figure 80.   The ideal wetsuit mitten for boating is precurved to fit around the paddle. The design shown was invented by the author.

Makeshift protection consists of light wool gloves under rubber dishwasher gloves and such; however, gloves and mittens cause loss of touch with the paddle. For kayakers and one-side canoe paddlers a recent invention is most helpful. Pogies ® are loose nylon gauntlets with open ends that attach around the paddle shaft with Velcro ® (figure 80). In a spill the Pogies stay on the paddle.

Neoprene mittens are also good protection but they must be made of one-eighth-inch material or thinner. The best mittens are made with a precurved hand.

Glasses. Dark glasses are often needed when paddling into the sun, and, of course, many paddlers must wear corrective lenses at all times. All glasses should be secured with a short length of cord or with a special glasses retaining strap.

Helmets. For kayaks, C-1's, and C-2's a helmet is a must (figure 81). It is optional in an open boat on easy water but highly recommended on Class III or IV water.

a

b

c

d

Figure 81. Four helmets for white water. Clockwise: (a) a rugged helmet specifically designed for boating, (b) a lighter weight boating helmet with excellent protection over the temples, (c) a rugged helmet but a little skimpy over the temples, and (d) an excellent buy. (The best hockey helmets, like this one, are good for boating. Avoid the cheap stuff.)

A good plastic helmet must be strong enough to survive a hard bash on a rock and be well retained by a chin strap. It should protect the temples as well as the top and back of the head, and, finally, it should redistribute and absorb energy.

The best helmets have a strap or flexible foam suspension system, but also have crushable foam to absorb energy. Suitable kinds are the best quality hockey helmets, rock climbing helmets, and helmets designed for white water. A good helmet

145

should drain quickly and not interfere with hearing. Some motorcycle helmets are also suitable.

Some people like to have a helmet with a visor or other face protection. It is more convenient, however, to make a habit of tucking the face and head against the chest with the body forward on the deck whenever one's decked boat is upside down.

Lifejackets. State laws require that there be one Coast Guard-approved lifejacket in the boat for every person (figure 82). Common sense requires that the jacket always be worn in white water.

Figure 82.   A good boating jacket has flotation all around and lots of it. For kayakers, it is often convenient to fold the section below the waist up over the top part of the jacket.

The most important aspect of a jacket is its comfort, for if it is uncomfortable, it won't be worn. For paddling, the flotation is best distributed all around the upper body in such a way that the arms are free. For kayaking, an additional requirement is that the jacket be short so as not to interfere with the spray skirt. Many jackets are provided with a break in the flotation at the waistline so the lower six inches of flotation can be folded up.

Buoyancy is also important in a lifejacket, especially on big water. Unfortunately, the large Coast Guard-approved jackets are not particularly good for paddling. The best compromise as this is written is the kit supplied by Wildwater Designs, Ltd.*

It provides almost twenty-five pounds of buoyancy *versus* 15.5 pounds for a standard jacket. As a kit it lacks approval; however, it is widely recognized, and if approval is a problem in a given area a cheap approved jacket can be carried along to please the authorities.

Figure 83. Typical 30 and 50 caliber ammunition boxes. Look for an intact gasket before buying these. For camera carrying pad the insides and add nylon lines for tying into the boat.

Dry Packs. Some kind of waterproof container is indispensable, even for short runs. In it you can carry not only spare clothing, but also a towel, food, maps, camera, and any other gear needing protection. Some makers of kayaks sell waterproof clothing bags, which are reliable but small. The most trustworthy container is a surplus 30 or 50 caliber ammunition box with an intact gasket (figure 83). With a little foam pad-

*Catalog of kits available from Wildwater Designs, Ltd., 230 Penllyn Pike, PA 19422.

147

ding, such an ammo box will bring a camera safely through the roughest circumstances. For expeditions large rubber packs are available, while flotation bags with removable ends are available for kayaks. For the occasional white water expedition, large white plastic pails can be gotten surplus from doughnut shops. One can also use heavy plastic trash bags securely tied and protected by a canvas bag or pack.

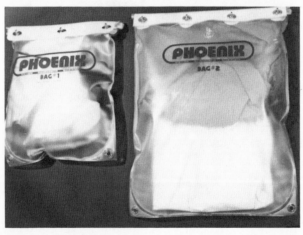

Figure 84. Plastic dry bags come in two styles. The bag above (a) has a plastic clamp that bends the open end around a rod to form a seal. In (b) a lip is rolled several times and then held in place by the snaps shown.

Camping Gear. For a sporty river section one often wants an unencumbered boat. When least loaded, your boat handles more easily and you need not worry about risking duffel in an upset. For this reason, as well as for efficient planning when time is limited, white water runs in the spring are often planned around campsites that are easily accessible by car. Thus there are no problems of weight or bulk involved. You ordinarily will need a sleeping bag, eating gear, tent, and other appropriate camping equipment. However, in the late spring and summer some paddlers organize more extended trips in which all gear and food are carried in the boats; weight and bulk now become important, and everything should be scrutinized with a backpacker's eye.

Canoe Paddles. Many types of canoe paddle are available (figure 85), but most are not suitable for white water. Ash makes the best solid wood paddle; however, the solid paddle has almost disappeared in favor of lighter, stronger paddles where each part is made of the best material for the purpose.

For moderately rocky water several good laminated wood paddles are available. Usually they are reinforced with aluminum at the tip or with a thin layer of fiberglass and plastic.

The ruggedest paddles have aluminum alloy shafts, glass-epoxy laminated blades, and plastic T-grip handles. The shaft is less cold to the grip if covered with plastic. Avoid paddles with polyester blades; they will not hold up well.

Canoe paddles can usually be judged by their price. Cheap paddles are a waste; however, an expensive paddle may be light but not rugged — so watch out.

For tandem paddling canoe paddles should be of moderate length. C-1's and C-2's require a paddle about one size shorter than normal, and soloing an open boat requires one size larger. If you must have a rule of thumb, start by trying a paddle that reaches the chin. It is best to borrow or rent paddles of several lengths before selecting the length that is right for you.

149

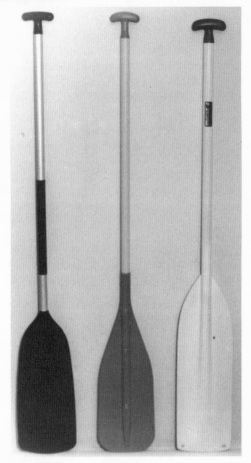

Figure 85.   Three white water paddles with tee grips. The paddle on the left is inexpensive and lacks the aluminum shaft inside the blade to reinforce it. The center paddle is ABS plastic. The one on the right is a fiberglass epoxy laminate with a reinforced tip.

Paddles also come with blades of greater or lesser area. While flat water racers like a huge blade area, a blade measuring between 7 and 9 inches wide and 22 to 25 inches long is usually about right for white water. Here again, sample different sized blades before purchasing the one best for you.

Kayak Paddles. The doubled-bladed kayak paddle is made with blades feathered — that is, set at right angles to one another. The feathered upper blade is less subject to wind and less exposed to spray flung at it when driving through heavy waves.

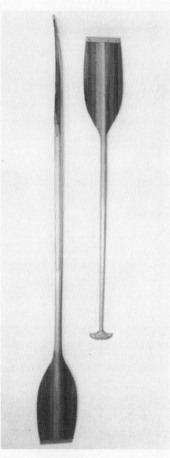

Figure 86. A typical reinforced epoxy-glass bladed kayak paddle of high quality.

Figure 87. These two beautiful laminated wood paddles represent the ultimate in high quality, light-weight white water paddles. Avoid using them in shallow, rocky river.

151

Paddles are made with both flat and lightly spooned blades. It is generally agreed that spooned blades require greater finesse in the bracing strokes, but that they have a compensatory advantage in power. Flat blades, on the other hand, are as effective backward as forward and avoid the risk of confusion from an inadvertently turned paddle. Spooned blades must be purchased as right hand-controlled or left.

To select a paddle of the correct size, place a paddle on your head in front of a mirror or another person and hold the elbows at right angles. The hands should clear the blades by an inch or two. A paddle with a typical 22-inch blade will be 82 or 84 inches long for an average person on an eastern river. For heavy western water use the next size up. Small or large persons will want to go one size smaller or larger.

Many paddles are made with laminated wood blades and reinforced tips, but those made with fiberglass blades and aluminum or wood shafts are more rugged than wood. Inexpensive paddles are a waste of money. An epoxy-glass blade with an aluminum alloy shaft or a carefully crafted laminated wood paddle cannot be made cheaply. For a spare paddle, take-apart shafts are available so the folded unit can be stowed under the stern flotation bag. Here again, avoid cheap paddles. One spare for a group of boats should be enough if everyone has a quality paddle at the start of a trip. More spares are in order on expedition paddle trips.

Throw Bag. The standard way to fish a boater out of a stream from the shore used to be with a coil of rope (see figure 88). Now there is a better way — the throw bag. It can be ordered from Charlie Walbridge of Wildwater Designs, Ltd., who has been its most ardent proponent — or the reader can make his own.

Start with 65 to 100 feet of ⅜-inch braided polypropylene line. (Polypropylene floats.) The length will depend on the rivers where it is to be used. Avoid a long line for use on narrow rivers where the extra line keeps getting in the way. The bag itself should be about five inches in diameter and about 10 inches high. Use heavy nylon pack fabric for easy stuffing of the line, or lighter fabric if you prefer. Place a hole in the center of the bottom panel for the line to pass through; reinforce it with a ⅜-inch grommet. Alternately the hole can be reinforced like a buttonhole. Place a draw string hem around the top and add sturdy string and a draw string clamp.

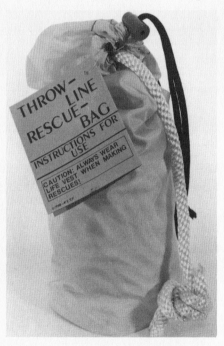

Figure 88.   A good throw bag should be of the shape shown. Use 65-100 feet of 3/8 or 7/16 polypropylene rope, which must be braided, not twisted.

The line is installed by making a loop on the end for the rescuer to hold and then passing the line up through the grommet. An optional piece of 2-inch-thick polyethylene foam is next followed by an overhand knot inside the bag. A knot on the far end is also recommended so the line will not slip away from the thrower.

Many boaters install a couple of short tie-in strings separate from the draw string, while others use a strap with a

153

Velcro ® fastener to accomplish the same thing. To be useful a throw rope should be instantly available.

After making a throw bag, practice using it. Also, practice the old fashioned method of coiling the line for heaving with half the coil in one hand and half in the other. The coil is preferred when a second rescue must be made before the bag can be restuffed. To stuff the bag, make a few small coils and stuff, a few more and stuff, and so on. Do *not* unkink any kinks that form by passing them to the end. Stuff them as they form. Then the line will pay out straight as each kink corrects the twists made by the coils as they went in.

WHITE WATER OPEN CANOES

Design Features of a Canoe. The design of a canoe, as of any boat, is the result of a carefully considered compromise in which the qualities of strength, weight, speed, maneuverability, and stability have been brought into the best balance for the intended use. For speed, a canoe should be narrow, round-bottomed, and have long and sharp ends. For stability, it should be beamy, with width carried well into bow and stern, and have a relatively flat bottom. For straight running and good handling in a wind, it should have a straight bottom line and a shallow keel carried well toward the ends. For maneuverability, a canoe should be short, and the bottom line should be raised toward bow and stern (this is called "rocker"); the ends should be blunt, there should be no keel, and the bottom should be nearly flat in cross-section. And, the lighter the canoe is, the more quickly it will respond, yet it must be strong enough to withstand all the normal stresses of the rapids.

It is evident from this that a canoe designed for traveling with good speed on open water will be seriously handicapped in rapids of any difficulty, and that a canoe designed for white water alone will be somewhat awkward in lake travel. A design intended as a compromise between these two uses will be adequate in all but the most demanding rapids and fair for lake travel. A good example of such a compromise is the standard aluminum canoe with a shoe keel substituted for the more usual tee keel.

Aluminum Open Canoes. The canvas-covered wooden canoe, beautiful though it is, is not recommended for white water, for a rocky river is too rough for it and frequent minor repairing will be needed. For general river use wood is excelled by aluminum and fiberglass, both of which are relatively indifferent to rough handling and unaffected by minor scatches and scrapes. They need no normal maintenance, and are fairly easy to repair. Aluminum has a greater tendency to stick on rocks than other materials. With extra ribs for strength and a shoe keel substituted at the factory for the standard keel, 17-foot aluminum canoes are widely used on white water.

ABS Plastic Open Canoes. The most recent addition to white water technology is the ABS plastic boat, which is vacuum-formed from a thick sandwich of ABS and vinyl plastic with a foam core. This plastic is almost indestructible in ordinary use, but a few cautions are in order. Most manufacturers consider that the foam gives the boat enough flotation. This is not so. You must add extra flotation for white water (see below). After several seasons the ends will wear thin and must be reinforced with an epoxy-glass patch. Finally, the boat should have three thwarts for support if it comes to rest against a rock. Most manufacturers will make extra thwarts available.

Decks for Open Canoes. For rapids heavy enough to swamp an open canoe, these boats can be fitted with watertight decks and spray skirts to provide a seal between the deck and the paddler. Decks have been made of waterproofed or coated fabrics, fiberglass, and aluminum. A deck may be designed for paddling single, double, or have three cockpits to give the option of either. For extended cruising, the center section may have a large zippered opening for easy loading of duffel. Lacing to a tie-down rail and heavy snaps are among the several methods which have been used to attach the fabric deck to the boat, but basic safety considerations require that it be so securely attached that it could never come loose in an upset to entangle the paddler. The skirts should be separable from the deck and held to the cockpit rim by an elasticized bottom which allows instant release. Decks with sewn-in sleeves can be more difficult to get out of and should be avoided as an unnecessary risk. One canoe maker — Grumman — now makes a fabric deck for use with its boats. This design uses a rubber flange for attachment under the outwale and has three cockpits with separable skirts.

OUTFITTING AN OPEN CANOE

Thwarts and Seats. A typical canoe comes with two seats and three thwarts. A boat with only a center thwart needs to have the extra thwarts added for white water. The gunwales of the boat are less likely to be damaged in an accident if the boat has enough thwarts.

Seats are often a problem, since they may have sharp edges that can catch a shoe or boot. Glue in a wooden wedge behind the sharp edge to prevent it from catching people's feet. Many clubs consider forward seats too dangerous and replace them with thwarts or with stainless steel bars bent to place the center at a good seating height.

Many solo paddlers add an extra thwart about a foot and a half behind the center thwart for support when it is desirable to paddle behind the center of the boat.

FLOTATION FOR OPEN BOATS

There are three types of flotation for open boats — foam blocks, air bags, and side flotation. All three have one point in common; they are useless unless they are secured firmly into the boat. Tie points can be installed for all three systems, as described under side flotation below.

Flotation has several functions. Most obvious is that it displaces water. A boat full of water weighs almost a ton and is almost unstoppable as it moves in a rapid current. If the boat is broadside as it contacts a rock, the ends will keep going and the boat will literally wrap around the rock. The more air and foam that replaces water, the less a swamped boat weighs and the higher it rides in the water. Any of the types of flotation will displace water when a boat swamps from water coming over the side.

Side Flotation. Swamping is only one of the hazards of white water. Boats often tip over suddenly when entering or leaving eddies, and here the location of flotation can make a big difference. If flotation is placed along the sides between the bottom of the boat and the gunwales, it will support the boat when it is on its side. Such a boat will tend to flip upside down full of air rather than sinking. Side flotation adds about ten pounds to a boat.

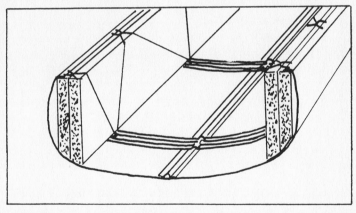

Figure 89.   Cross-section of a typical canoe with the flotation in place. The rib clips are almost hidden by the foam.

Polyethylene foam is lashed into a canoe as shown in figure 89. The sheets of foam are two inches thick and six feet long, with the height as shown. For an aluminum boat stainless steel clips can be made of one-sixteenth-inch diameter stainless steel welding rod and installed through the ribs and gunwales as shown in figure 90. Typically one needs five rib clips and six gunwale clips on each side.

 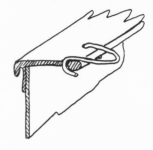

Figure 90. Stainless steel clip is inserted a rib cross-sectional view. Dotted lines show shape of clip prior to installation.

Tying into an ABS plastic or a fiberglass reinforced plastic boat is more difficult. The Blue Hole Canoe Company supplies self adhesive D-rings for installing tie-ins, or one may use the glass and epoxy tie-ins described here.

The following supplies are needed for 10 tie-ins:
    70 inches of 2-inch-wide fiberglass tape
    120 inches of 1-inch-wide fiberglass tape
    Epoxy kit, ½-pound or 1-pound
    15 inches of ¼-inch inside diameter polyethylene
    tubing
They can be obtained at marine supply or hardware dealers.

For side flotation the tie points should be spaced evenly about 14.5 inches apart and one inch underneath the foam. Mark each tie point and sand an area 3 x 6 inches clean. The tie point is laid up all at one time, with epoxy mixed to the manufacturer's directions. Mix only a little at a time. Keep this toxic guck off your hands. Apply it with a brush or scrap foam squeegee and wash up thoroughly afterward.

Wet out the boat, and then place down a 2 x 2-inch piece of glass tape and cover it with a 2 x 5-inch piece. Next place a 1½-inch piece of tubing down in the center of the glass and running parallel to the keel. Finally cover the tube with 3-, 4-, and 5-inch pieces of 1-inch-wide glass. Wet each piece out as you proceed. Cover the whole works with Handiwrap or other cheap plastic wrap (not Saran Wrap, which will stick). The wrap allows you to press out all air bubbles and excess resin. Remove the excess by lifting a corner and using a paper towel to wipe it up.

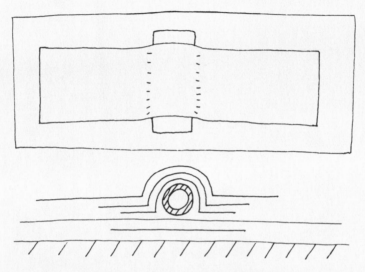

Figure 91.   Top and side view of a tie point. The polyethylene tube is 1.5 inches long with a 2- and a 5-inch piece of 2-inch-wide glass tape underneath and 3-, 4- and 5-inch pieces of one-inch-wide tape over the top.

The gunwale lashings for an ABS boat are best done by drilling two holes 1½ inches apart just below the gunwale. Do not drill the gunwale; it's already the weakest part of the boat. Make the holes just big enough to accommodate 1/8-inch diameter nylon line. To thread the line, heat an area near the end gently in a flame and cut it in half after it shrinks and melts slightly.

Foam Blocks. Large blocks of styrene foam can be gotten from a marine dealer. The blocks are notched to fit under the thwarts. To equip a boat for tandem and solo use, place a block so it just fits under the center and rear thwarts and solo the boat backwards by kneeling behind the center thwart. Foam

159

blocks tend to shed bits of foam, which are fatal when swallowed by certain species of fish. If you care about the environment, cover the blocks or don't use them.

Air Bags. The truck inner tube is a popular form of air bag. If it is not properly secured, it is useless. Some canoe suppliers have vinyl bags big enough for open boats. They can be secured under wood slats lashed between two thwarts.

Figure 92. This large air bag comes with grommets in the four corners to lash it in place. Pads such as those described for side flotation above are recommended for the lashing points.

For a description of side air bags see "Sausage Flotation for Open Boats" in *American Whitewater* (Vol. XXV, No. 2, March-April, 1980). A full description of foam flotation for an aluminum canoe can be found in Vol. XVIII, No. 1, Spring, 1973.

Ropes and Painters. A painter on each end of a canoe can be of great help during a boat rescue or if it is necessary to line the boat around an unrunnable section of river. The best painters are of 3/8-inch diameter polypropylene rope, which is thick enough to hold and light enough to float. When not in use painters must be secured to the decks so they cannot wrap around a boater's neck or leg during a spill. Use a short piece of shock cord attached to the deck at both ends to hold the painter.

Pads for Kneeling. Many persons prefer knee pads, but foam padding permanently installed in the boat has much to commend it. Solo paddlers often use foam pads with sockets for the knees for extra stability.

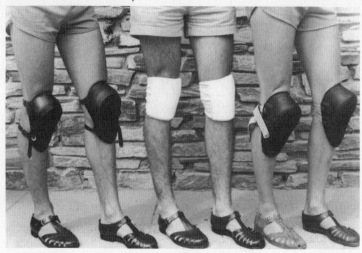

Figure 93. Knee pads. Left to right: the mason's or gardener's knee pad is inexpensive and good. The basketball player's knee pad slides around too much for many people. The super pads here are made for miners. They are extra heavy but will last a long time.

KAYAKS, C-1'S, AND C-2'S

Design Compromises. The design of a kayak or C-1 involves the same set of compromises as that for an open canoe (figures 94 and 95). Strength, weight, speed, stability, and maneuverability must all be reconciled in the final form. Width, or beam, is a consideration peculiar to the kayak for two reasons. In the first place, the paddler sits low and uses a relatively short

161

double paddle; a wide hull would make the paddle strokes awkward. More important, present-day kayak technique is based upon strong leans in turning and crossing currents.

Figure 94.   A typical maneuverable kayak for river running. A slalom boat would be more pointed at the ends and thinner except in the middle.

Figure 95.   A cruising C-1 of relatively high volume. The boat shown here is rotationally molded in one piece of high-density polyethylene plastic.

New Technologies. Kayaks and the decked C-1 and C-2 canoes are coming to look more and more alike, especially the boats built for slalom racing. These boats all share a common technology that began with the laying up of boats made of fiberglass and polyester resin in the early sixties. Good boats of this type are made of glass cloth, while poor boats are mostly mat and should be avoided.

The molds for laid up boats are relatively inexpensive, so boat designs have evolved quickly, with boats of many special types now available (see below). Many clubs have molds available so a boater can build his own craft.

The most recent improvements in boat building have been made possible by the availability of new lightweight fibers. Several deserve particular mention. Kevlar, DuPont's brand of aramid fiber, has the strength and stiffness of steel with the density of nylon. Nylon has great strength but stretches easily. Dacron polyester is a stiffer fabric in a lay up, and polypropylene is in between but close to nylon. The finest lightweight boats use vinyl ester resin and Kevlar combined with other lightweight fabrics and with S-glass. Stiffening ribs can be added from ultra-stiff carbon fiber or the stiffness can be achieved by thicker ribs with foam cores. Expect to pay almost twice as much for a high technology boat by a good designer and builder.

Another new technology for boat building is rotational molding. Here an entire boat with no seams is formed by tumbling powered plastic in a hot metal mold. These "Tupperware" boats are made of high density polyethylene and are very rugged. They are almost impossible to repair, however, if they are holed through. Boats of this type lack stiffness and require foam bulkheads (see below).

Three Types of Kayak and C-1. There are three basic styles of kayak and C-1. Slalom boats are very thin top to bottom, especially in the stern. They have considerable rocker fore and aft for ease in turning, and they are uncomfortable to stay in for long periods.

For wild water or straight downriver racing, only speed is important so a long thin boat with a V-bottom is desirable. The stern of a typical wild water racer looks angular and dartlike.

163

For general maneuvering in complex rapids a compromise boat with a little more room than a slalom boat is wanted. Otherwise, the general purpose boat is much like a slalom boat.

For racing, kayaks must be at least sixty centimeters wide and C-1's seventy centimeters. The minimum length is four meters for slalom boats and the maximum is 4.5 meters for wild water. Wild water C-1's must be at least eighty centimeters wide and no longer than 4.3 meters. For slalom, a C-2 is eighty centimeters wide by at least fifteen feet (4.58 meters) long. Wild water C-2's are eighty centimeters wide by no more than five meters long.

OUTFITTING A KAYAK

Seat. Commercially built kayaks come with premolded seats that are usually suspended from and integral with the cockpit rim. Be sure to sit in the seat of any boat before purchasing it. It may not fit you. A seat that is too wide can be padded with polyethylene foam glued on with good quality contact cement or with scraps of wetsuit material. There should be no sideways motion of your buttocks with respect to the kayak seat when you bend from side to side at the waist.

Knee Braces. Some kayaks are configured so that there are pockets for the knees and thighs. High volume boats often have built-in plastic braces, and braces are often made integral with the seat-rim assembly. Here again, test a boat ahead of time. If you can't rock from side to side without your knees sliding around, you will need to add padding as with the seat. In extreme cases the foam padding may have to be of an impractical shape that must be covered with glass cloth and resin for strength.

Foot Braces. It is very difficult to hold your knees in place when your feet are free to move. Toe blocks are the answer. The simplest block is a foam piece of triangular cross-section covered with layers of cloth and resin. Much better but a bit heavier are the adjustable braces that can be installed by anyone who can mark and drill a couple of holes. The best are made by The Wheels of Industry (formerly Yakima Products) (figure 96), but there are other good ones available. The blocks should be located on the sides at about seam level on most boats.

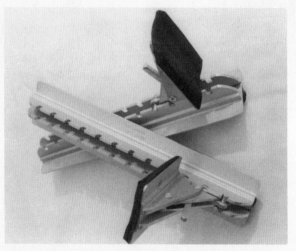

Figure 96. These adjustable kayak foot braces can be installed in a few minutes by anyone with an electric drill.

Grab Loops and Painters. Grab loops at both ends of a boat are a must. If they are missing, they must be installed. Without loops you cannot self-rescue the boat after a spill and you cannot properly secure it for car topping. Bow painters are a nuisance and will catch the paddle during a roll. A short stern painter held to the deck by a piece of shock cord just behind the cockpit on one side is useful if you expect another boater to rescue your boat when you let go of it after a spill. It is easy to paddle with a short painter held in one's teeth.

Longitudinal Walls. Walls of two-inch-thick polyethylene foam are often added to lightweight boats to add strength. Typically, in a kayak these bulkheads run from the bow to the

165

feet and from behind the cockpit to the stern. Avoid a wall in front between your feet unless you have small feet. Why take a chance with caught feet! To add walls to a boat, follow the procedure below for a perfect fit. You will need two people, one to hold the boat and a second to mark and measure.

1. Place the boat on its side on top of the piece of foam or on top of a sheet of paper to be used as a cutting template.

2. The boat should be reasonably level fore and aft and the two edges of the cockpit should be vertical. A large carpenter's layout square will enable you to get the cockpit edges square with the floor. Alternatively use a plumb bob. Hold the boat so it cannot move.

3. Take a small plumb bob and hold the cord against the center of the deck at the bow and mark the point where the bob touches the foam. Move from the end of the boat toward the cockpit and then do the same thing for the hull. The marks will enable the foam to be cut exactly to fit. Check the ends several times with the bob while marking to make sure the boat hasn't moved. Cut the foam with a sharp kitchen knife.

4. Look at the deck. You may have to round the top edge of the foam for a good fit. Then force the foam into place.

You will need to secure the foam in place for maximum effectiveness and safety. Use blocks of foam contact-cemented to sanded areas next to the foam. Such blocks can be easily gotten off should the boat require foam removal during repairs.

Flotation Bags. As built, a kayak will sink or float almost under the surface of the water. Extra flotation is a necessity for a small light boat to survive a trip through the rocks (figure 97). Full of water, the boat weighs about a quarter of a ton and will smash itself to pieces. Full of air, it floats on the water and only has its original mass and momentum when it hits an obstruction.

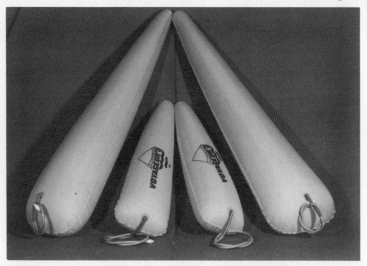

Figure 97. Split air bags are placed on either side of an Ethafoam ® bulkhead, with the small bags up front forward of the foot braces and the large bags in back of the seats. For a C-1, buy four of the long bags.

The best practice is to place full-length flotation bags behind the seat reaching to the stern and short bags in the bow in front of the paddler's feet. For boats with foam bulkheads, split bags must be used even though the cost is higher. Note that several companies make bags with removable ends so that gear can be carried inside. Full-strength bags are .020 inch thick (20 mils), while lightweight bags are thinner. Sit bags are made of heat-sealed vinyl.

Before installing air bags in a new or modified boat, carefully inspect the inside for sharp projections that might puncture the bag, and blunt or remove them.

Spray Skirts. The spray skirt provides a watertight seal between the paddler and cockpit rim (figure 98). Here fit is more important than what the skirt is made of. A typical skirt is a waterproof fabric or stretch neoprene sheet with a tubular waist section held around the kayaker's waist by a separate elastic cord or the stretch action of the neoprene. The outer edge of the skirt contains an elastic cord, usually one-quarter-inch shock cord that holds it in place on the cockpit rim.

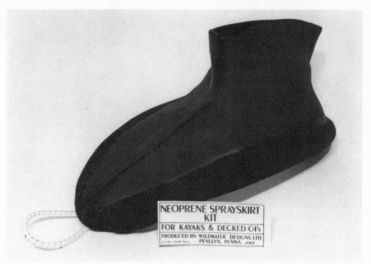

Figure 98.   A neoprene ® spray skirt made from a Walbridge kit. The perfect fit available from a kit is rarely found in a dealer-supplied skirt.

The ideal skirt will be almost tight in front of the boater when it is in place on the rim, so that water does not puddle and push the skirt down. The biggest problem with neoprene skirts is that people think they can be stretched to fit a rim that is larger than the skirt. It is all right to stretch a skirt a quarter of an inch or so — but no more either sideways or front to back. A good fit at the waist for a neoprene skirt occurs when the skirt opening circumference is eighty-five percent of the boater's waist measurement. You should be able to thump your fist on the center of the skirt without its popping off. It is better to do this test with the skirt wet and slippery.

Be very suspicious when you purchase a boat from a dealer. The dealer does not want to be stuck with skirts of many sizes, so he will often try to convince you that one skirt will fit any boat in his showroom.

If you cannot find a skirt that fits or if you want a less expensive skirt that is top quality, consult Charlie Walbridge's *Boat Builder's Manual* or order one of his kits. Some dealers stock the Walbridge kits.

OUTFITTING A C-1 OR C-2

Much of what has been written above about the kayak applies to the modern C-1 and C-2, which come closer to the kayak in design than they do to an open canoe. When appropriate read the section above for a more detailed discussion.

Seat. There are three styles in C-1 seats — molded, sling, and foam. A molded seat is an extension of the cockpit rim. It is losing favor as boats are being made smaller, because it is too easy to get a foot caught by it. A sling seat is sewn from heavy nylon fabric, with a tunnel for a heavy cord or wire. It requires a cockpit rim big enough to accommodate both the cord and the spray skirt. The sling covers the rear quarter or third of the cockpit. The corners are often riveted to the cockpit for extra stability.

The most popular seat for C-1's and C-2's is made of two or three two-inch thicknesses of polyethylene foam. To laminate the foam, use contact cement or, even better, heat the two surfaces with an industrial "hair drier" and stick them together hot. (Practice this with scrap foam first.) Use the narrowest seat that is comfortable.

Foam seats are of two general types. They may start about six inches under the rear deck and come forward even with the crotch, or they may come all the way forward and wedge under the forward deck. Seats are often keyed to lock around foam bulkheads under the decks. The advantages of the longer seat are that it can be used to hold the lower end of the thigh straps in place and that it is less likely to come loose. Whether the seat comes with the boat or you build it, it needs to fit you. With a

169

sharp knife carve the seat to fit. Pay particular attention to the area between the legs so the blood in the femoral arteries is not pinched off.

A foam seat must be held in place somehow. If the structure of the boat doesn't wedge it into place, contact cement foam blocks in place or make polyester-glass L-brackets.

Thigh Straps. You don't want to fall out of the boat when upside down, so thigh straps will be needed. These straps are usually two inches wide and run from the center of the boat just in front of the crotch to attachment points on either side. These points are glassed-in pieces of braided nylon rope or screwed-in metal fittings close to the cockpit rim and just behind the hip joints. The center attachment point is a glassed-in length of rope or a piece of aluminum tube notched into an elongated foam seat. The straps should be adjustable. Some boaters use aluminum "straps" referred to as "machines" for the ultimate in stability. They are hazardous and at least one boater came close to losing his life because he had machines instead of nylon web straps.

Skirts. A canoeist's waist is higher than the deck of the boat, so the skirt must rise in a gentle arch from the front center cockpit rim to the waistline. There must also be extra room on the sides, and the boater must be able to lean all the way forward on the deck without the back of the skirt popping off.

Toe and Ankle Blocks. It is easier to stay locked into the boat if the toes can push against toe blocks. In very low-volume boats, a foam pad under the ankles will increase comfort. Toe blocks can be foam-covered with glass and resin or they can be elaborate adjustable aluminum affairs that are glassed in. Always consider getting toes off of the blocks for a quick escape when designing a toe block system. The decisions about toe and ankle blocks relate to safety, stability, and how much sheer pain the boater can endure. For C-1 and C-2 paddlers, true comfort is almost unknown. Just try to avoid unbearable pain.

Knee Pads. Never wear strapped-on knee pads with thigh straps. Instead, glue foam pads into the boat at the appropriate places.

Grab Loops, Longitudinal Walls, and Flotation Bags. For these items read the section on kayak outfitting above.

CARRYING BOATS ON AN AUTOMOBILE

Car-Topping Canoes. Canoes are easily carried on car-top carriers. Bolt a six-foot wooden crossbar to a standard rack to carry two canoes. Use eye bolts at the ends of the crossbars and set into the front and rear bumpers for attachment of the tie-down lines; most bumpers have sharp lower edges which will cut through any line after a short time. For secure attachment, tie the boat fore and aft to the bumpers, and use straps or lines over the boat as well. Never depend upon attachment to the rack alone. Canoes have been blown off cars on the highway.

Figure 99. The style of clamp-on rack shown here is best for cars that have strong rain gutters.

Use extra care in choosing a rack for a compact car. Rain gutters are now small or nonexistent and the supports must be matched to the strength of the roof and the attachment points. Racks should not extend beyond the width of the widest portion of the car as required by most state laws, and the ends should be rounded or padded to prevent bruised heads.

Kayak and C-1 Carriers. Special racks are available with saddles for carrying kayaks and C-1's. Alternatively, a saddle can be cut from polyethylene foam and attached to a wooden rack. The foam saddle is easier to shift around than the more permanent saddles sold with racks. Many kayakers use an upright piece of wood near the center of a wooden rack to aid in stacking kayaks next to each other on their sides. A kayak on its side is less likely to be damaged by the rack than one on its bottom. For best results, side-stacked kayaks should also be provided with contoured saddles.

REPAIRING CANOES AND KAYAKS

Fixing a Canoe on the River. When a boat has been damaged on the river, it is likely that some careful repair work will be necessary after the trip, yet repair on the bank often will allow continuing.

An aluminum or ABS plastic canoe which has been swamped on a rock may have the bottom crushed in amidships, so that it is at the level of the gunwales. After it has been brought in and emptied, it can often be restored to a fair imitation of its former self by placing it in shallow water and jumping up and down on the bulge. Do not jump on it on land, for this can damage it further.

Small breaks in the skin, pulled rivets, and other leaks can be patched on the spot with duct tape or other plastic tape with a strong adhesive coating. Tape must be applied to the outside of the hull to get a good seal, and it is vulnerable to being scraped off. Tape can be applied only to a dry surface. The prudent boater carries both tape and a few paper towels in a waterproof container.

Fixing a Bent Aluminum Canoe. To put the shape back into a bent aluminum boat, the metal must be reformed. To do this, turn the craft upside down over a wooden post. Have one or two people push down on each end of the canoe so that the post forces the bottom of the boat back close to its original position.

When the metal is approximately correct, tap the area where the post is in contact and the area immediately around it with a heavy rock or a mason's hammer. The first application of this stretch-and-set technique will not seem to do too much; but, as the post is repositioned over each pushed-in area in turn, the boat will gradually return to its proper shape.

If the post is high enough, the side of the canoe can be placed over the post with the gunwale in contact and bent gunwales straightened. Gunwales, ribs, and keel will all respond to stretch-and-set if the team doing the work is patient.

Note that the hammering is used to reset the metal. Avoid blows that are so heavy that they further stretch the metal.

Patching an Aluminum Hull. The best permanent repair to a crack in an aluminum hull is an aluminum patch riveted into place. Aircraft rivets with countersunk heads are required so that the patch will be flush. Grumman canoe dealers will usually obtain rivets and replacement parts when needed, but the nuisance value to the dealer is high. It is best if canoe clubs or one dealer in an area stock repair material. Patches are made from 6061-T6 alloy of .050- or .063-inch thickness.

For a simple crack, the patch should be about two inches wide and extend an inch beyond the crack on either end. Round the ends of the patch. It will be placed on the inside of the boat. A complex cracked area may result in metal that is so distorted that an area in the middle must be removed and a larger patch used. Drill a small hole at the end of each crack to prevent it from propagating after the patch is in place.

Drilling for a Patch. A supply of steel machine screws and nuts must be available for temporary use when patching. One-eighth-inch diameter screws are best. Number 6 screws are too large and number 4 screws will break. Form the patch and place it over the damaged area. Drill two holes on a line running parallel to the long axis of the boat and about three-eights of an inch from the edge of the patch. These go all the way through the patch and hull. Secure the patch with two screws. Drill additional holes about three-quarters of an inch apart and screw the patch down as often as is required to keep it flat against the hull. Work away from the original two holes, first one way and then the other. The patch is screwed flat so that all holes will line up perfectly when the patch is later applied. One cannot drill holes after putting sealer between the hull and the patch.

Sealing the Patch. Remove all the screws and apply a sealer between the patch and the hull. Glazing compound or any of the high-quality oil-based caulking compounds used for wood frame buildings make good seals. For a large patch, do not use silicone rubber. It will set up before the patch is complete and will keep the rivets from pulling the patch up against the hull.

Riveting. Use a countersink to prepare the holes in the hull for the rivet heads. The countersinking is done from the outside for an inside patch. Use great care to get the right size countersink. Practice on a scrap of patch first. The rivets are set by holding a heavy steel bar or hammer head against the rivet head while a second person hits the end of the rivet inside the boat with a light hammer. It is sufficient to thicken the end of the rivet. It need not be squashed flat. Install rivets in the same order as the holes were drilled. Use screws to hold the patch flat while riveting.

Breaks in the metal should never be welded. The aluminum alloy used for canoes has been heat-treated after forming, and if welded it develops a brittle area surrounded by an annealed or soft portion. Such a weld not only has very little strength but also has a high probability of cracking.

PATCHING PLASTIC BOATS

Theory of a Successful Patch. Most people would prefer to glue a patch over a crack or damaged area and be done with it. It won't work. Not only will patches of this sort add unnecessary weight to a boat, but they will also lead to new cracks right over the old ones. It is easy to see why. Suppose the patch is the same thickness as the hull. Everywhere the patch has been added is now thicker and stiffer than before, so all flexion must occur at the only thin point, the crack. The result is inevitable, another crack. Of course, in an emergency a poor patch is better than none at all. With polyester resin and a stove, it is possible to do a major emergency patch in about forty minutes.

For a strong patch the hull must be made thinner around the crack. Grind away hull material until the hull is paper thin at the crack and tapers to full thickness an inch to an inch-and-a-half away. The patch is added full thickness in the center and thinner toward the outside. The best grinding tool is a 5- or 6-inch diameter disc for a drill, such as Sears Extra Course sanding discs. Anything less coarse will fill up with plastic.

Fiberglass Patches. The best patches for either fiberglass or ABS plastic boats are made from epoxy and fiberglass. Use ten-ounce glass cloth and an epoxy formulated for boat work. Both are available from marine dealers. For a fiberglass boat, the center of the patch should have as many thicknesses as the original hull. Cut the inner strip quite narrow, the next wider, and so on. A typical patch would have strips a half inch, an inch, an inch and a half, and two inches wide. Be sure that the area around the heavy grinding is sanded lightly so the patch can overlap somewhat.

For a perfect patch mix enough resin for one patch at a time. Wet out the hull first, and then add strips one at a time, wetting out each in turn. Avoid excess resin. Cover the finished patch with Handiwrap or other inexpensive food wrap (not Saran Wrap). Gentle pressure over the wrap will consolidate the patch and push bubbles and excess resin out to the sides where it can be removed by lifting an edge and wiping with a paper towel. Finally, pull the wrap tight with strips of masking tape for a patch that has a glass-like surface. The wrap is stripped off after the patch has set.

Patching kits are often available from dealers for the boats they sell. They may work well, but then again they may not. Avoid any kit that does not come with clear and adequate instructions.

A polyester-fiberglass boat can be patched using polyester resin. The bond is not as good as with epoxy, but the material is less expensive and it can be mixed so that it sets up within a short time, especially if heated. Epoxy patches need at least twelve hours to cure. Both types of resin are toxic and require adequate ventilation as well as protection for the hands. Wash all chemicals off quickly with strong soap and water. Boraxo is good.

APPENDIX A

Knots

Among the subsidiary skills, knot tying is a necessary one for any boater. He must attach a line to his boat and to the shore. He may need to join two lines when lining his boat or hauling out a swamped canoe — or a stuck car. And, he must tie his boat to his car with absolute security.

Avoid the square knot, except for trivial uses. Like any knot based on the overhand knot, it will jam under load. It is not secure if used for joining ropes of different sizes, and it upsets if the pull comes on the wrong part.

Of the many dozens of useful knots, the handful described here will serve nearly every need.

Sheet Bend. (Fig. 100) Secure, easy to tie, and useful for joining ropes of different sizes or materials. Caution: the free ends must be on the same side, as shown. When they are on opposite sides, the bend can slip. Under great loads, the sheet bend can jam. For this use the Carrick bend, below.

Figure 100.

Double Sheet Bend. (Fig. 101) More secure than the single sheet bend, and should be used when rope sizes are much dissimilar.

Figure 101.

Carrick Bend. (Figures 102 and 103) A strong, secure, and jam-proof means of joining two lines. Form a loop in one hand. With the other hand lay the second line over the loop and form the interlaced pattern of figure 102. When pulled tight, this bend "upsets" to the form shown in figure 103. Since a good deal of slip occurs during the process of upsetting, make the ends longer than those shown in figure 102. Caution: several inferior forms of this knot are possible if the over-and-under pattern is not followed exactly; if the free ends are on the same side, rather than on opposite sides as shown, a less secure knot will result.

Figure 102.   *Figure 103.*

Bowline. (Figs. 104 and 105) The old standby whenever you need a loop. Does not slip or jam, and is secure. Form the loop in one hand, then pass the free end through, around the standing part, then back through the loop as shown. Notice that the form of the bowline is identical with that of the sheet bend. For maximal security, the loop, or cuckold's neck, may be doubled, as in the double sheet bend (figure 101). Two ropes are often tied together with a bowline in each one.

Figure 104.   *Figure 105.*

Clove Hitch. (Fig. 106) A quick and relatively secure attachment of a line to a spar or mooring post. If used at the end of a line, a half hitch should be taken with the free end around the standing part.

Figure 106.

Rolling Hitch. (Figs. 107, 108, and 109) Also called the midshipman's hitch, or tautline hitch. This is a hitch of many uses, since it can be taken in a line under tension, and can be adjusted by sliding up and down the line. Take a half hitch around the standing part, then return with the free end inside the first turn, as in figure 107. This second turn wedged inside the first is

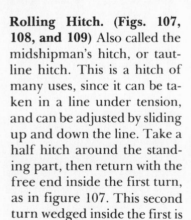

Figure 107.

179

the heart of this hitch, as it kinks the standing part when a load is applied. This hitch can be finished off in a variety of ways, but the most convenient is a half hitch on the standing part, as shown in figure 108. Figure 109 shows the hitch pulled tight.

Figure 108.

Figure 109.

Figure 110.

Butterfly Noose. (Figures 110, 111, and 112) Used by climbers for the attachment of pitons or as a middle loop in a climbing rope. It is secure, cannot jam, and will accommodate a load in any direction. Several of these loops will allow spaced points of purchase for a winch in hauling a swamped boat out of a river, or will provide convenient and secure holds for several men in hauling on a line, and so on. To tie it, twist a loop in the bight (figure 110), then fold up the lower part of the loop and pull it through the center (figure 111) Figure 112 shows the completed knot.

Figure 111.   *Figure 112.*

APPENDIX B

American Whitewater Affiliation Safety Code

Revised 1980

A guide to safe river boating in canoe, kayak, or raft. Prepared and published by the **American Whitewater Affiliation,** a volunteer organization of paddlers and clubs interested in white water sport, and publishers of the bimonthly *American Whitewater Journal,* which offers not only entertainment but also up-to-date information on techniques, equipment, safety, conservation, racing, and river access developments, as well as a complete listing of affiliated clubs and how to contact them.

For further information write to:

> **American Whitewater Affiliation**
> **Safety Codes**
> **P.O. Box 1261**
> **Jefferson City, MO 65102**

I. PERSONAL PREPAREDNESS AND RESPONSIBILITY

1. BE A COMPETENT SWIMMER with ability to handle yourself underwater.

2. WEAR A LIFEJACKET.

3. KEEP YOUR CRAFT UNDER CONTROL. Control must be good enough at all times to stop or reach shore before you reach any danger. Do not enter a rapids unless you are reasonably sure you can safely navigate it, or swim the entire rapids in the event of a capsize.

4. BE AWARE OF RIVER HAZARDS AND AVOID THEM. Following are the most frequent KILLERS:

   a. *HIGH WATER.* The river's power and danger and the difficulty of rescue increase tremendously as the flow rate increases. It is often misleading to judge river level at the put-in. Look at a narrow critical passage. Could a *sudden* rise from sun on a snow pack, rain, or a dam release occur on your trip?

   b. *COLD.* Cold quickly robs one's strength, along with his will and ability to save himself. Dress to protect yourself from cold water and weather extremes. When the water temperature is less than 50° F., a diver's wetsuit is essential for safety in the event of an upset. Next best is wool clothing under a windproof outer garment such as a splash-proof nylon shell; in this case, one should also carry matches and a complete change of clothes in a waterproof package. If, after prolonged exposure, a person experiences uncontrollable shaking or has difficulty talking and moving, he must be warmed immediately by whatever means available.

   c. *STRAINERS.* Brush, fallen trees, bridge pilings, or anything else which allows the river currents to sweep through but pins boat and boater against the obstacle. The water pressure on anything trapped this way is overwhelming, and there may be little or no white water to warn of danger.

   d. *WEIRS, REVERSALS, AND SOUSE HOLES.* The water drops over an obstacle, then curls back on itself in a stationary wave, as is often seen at weirs and dams. The surface water is actually going UPSTREAM, and this action will trap any floating object between the drop

183

---

and the wave. Once trapped, a swimmer's only hope is to dive below the surface where the current is flowing downstream, or to try to swim out the end of the wave.

5. BOATING ALONE is not recommended. The preferred minimum is three craft.

6. HAVE A FRANK KNOWLEDGE OF YOUR BOATING ABILITY. Don't attempt waters beyond this ability. Learn paddling skills and teamwork, if in a multiple-manned craft, to match the river you plan to boat.

7. BE IN GOOD PHYSICAL CONDITION consistent with the difficulties that may be expected.

8. BE PRACTICED IN ESCAPE from an overturned craft, in self rescue, in rescue and in ARTIFICIAL RESPIRATION. Know first aid.

9. THE ESKIMO ROLL should be mastered by kayakers and canoers planning to run large rivers and/or rivers with continuous rapids where a swimmer would have trouble reaching shore.

10. WEAR A CRASH HELMET where an upset is likely. This is essential in a kayak or covered canoe.

11. BE SUITABLY EQUIPPED. Wear shoes that will protect your feet during a bad swim, or a walk for help, yet will not interfere with swimming (tennis shoes recommended). Carry a knife and waterproof matches. If you need eyeglasses, tie them on and carry a spare pair. Do not wear bulky clothing that will interfere with your swimming ability when waterlogged.

II. BOAT AND EQUIPMENT PREPAREDNESS

1. TEST NEW AND UNFAMILIAR EQUIPMENT before relying on it for difficult runs.

2. BE SURE CRAFT IS IN GOOD REPAIR before starting on a trip. Eliminate sharp projections that could cause injury during a swim.

3. Inflatable craft should have MULTIPLE AIR CHAM-BERS, and should be test-inflated before starting trip.

4. HAVE STRONG, ADEQUATELY SIZED PADDLE OR OARS for controlling the craft, and carry sufficient spares for the length of the trip.

5. INSTALL FLOTATION DEVICES in non-inflatable craft, securely fixed and designed to displace as much water from the craft as possible.

6. BE CERTAIN THERE IS ABSOLUTELY NOTHING TO CAUSE ENTANGLEMENT when coming free from an upset craft, i.e., a spray skirt that won't release or tangles around legs; lifejacket buckles or clothing that might snag; canoe seats that lock on shoe heels; foot braces that fail or allow feet to jam under them; flexible decks that collapse on boater's legs when a kayak is trapped by water pressure; baggage that dangles in an upset; loose rope in the craft or badly secured bow/stern lines.

7. PROVIDE ROPES TO ALLOW YOU TO HOLD ONTO YOUR CRAFT in case of upset, and so that it may be rescued. Following are the recommended methods:

   a. KAYAKS AND COVERED CANOES should have 6-inch diameter grab loops of 1/4-inch rope attached to bow and stern. A strern painter 7 or 8 feet long is optional and may be used if properly secured to prevent entanglement.

   b. OPEN CANOES should have bow and stern lines (painters) securely attached, consisting of 8 to 10 feet of 1/4- or 3/8-inch rope. These lines must be secured in such a way that they will not come loose accidentally and entangle the boaters during a swim, yet they must be ready for immediate use during an emergency. Attached balls, floats, and knots are *NOT* recommended.

   c. RAFTS AND DORIES should have taut perimeter grab lines threaded through the loops usually provided.

8. RESPECT RULES FOR RAFT CAPACITY and know how these capacities should be reduced for white water use. Liferaft ratings must generally be halved.

9. CARRY APPROPRIATE REPAIR MATERIALS; tape (heating duct tape) for short trips and complete repair kit for wilderness trips.

10. CARTOP RACKS MUST BE STRONG and positively attached to the vehicle, and each boat must be tied to each rack. In addition, each end of each boat should be tied to the car bumper. Suction cup racks are poor. The entire arrangement should be able to withstand all but the most violent vehicle accident.

III. LEADER'S PREPAREDNESS AND RESPONSIBILITY

1. RIVER CONDITIONS. Have a reasonable knowledge of the difficult parts of the run or, if an exploratory trip, examine maps to estimate the feasibility of the run. Be aware of possible rapid changes in river levels and how these changes can affect the difficulty of the run. If important, determine the approximate flow rate or level. If the trip involves important tidal currents, secure tide information.

2. PARTICIPANTS. Inform participants of expected river conditions and determine if the prospective boaters are qualified for the trip. All decisions should be founded on group safety and comfort. Difficult decisions on the participation of marginal boaters must be based on total group strength.

3. EQUIPMENT. Plan so that all necessary group equipment is present on the trip; 50- to 100-foot throwing rope, first aid kit with fresh and adequate supplies, extra paddles, repair materials, and survival equipment if appropriate. Check equipment as necessary at the put-in, especially: lifejackets, boat flotation, and any item that could prevent complete escape from the boat in case of an upset.

4. ORGANIZATION. Remind each member of individual responsibility in keeping group compact and intact between the leader and sweep (capable rear boat). If group is too large, divide into smaller groups, each of appropriate boating strength, and designate group leaders and sweeps.

5. FLOAT PLAN. If the trip is into a wilderness area, or for an extended period, your plans should be filed with appropriate authorities or left with someone who will contact them after a certain time. Establishment of checkpoints along the way, at which civilization could be contacted if necessary, should be considered. Knowing the location of possible help could speed rescue in any case.

IV. IN CASE OF UPSET

1. EVACUATE YOUR BOAT IMMEDIATELY if there is imminent danger of being trapped against logs, brush, or any other form of strainer.

2. RECOVER WITH AN ESKIMO ROLL IF POSSIBLE.

3. IF YOU SWIM, HOLD ON TO YOUR CRAFT — it has much flotation and is easy for rescuers to spot. Get to the upstream end so craft cannot crush you against obstacles.

4. RELEASE YOUR CRAFT IF THIS IMPROVES YOUR SAFETY. If rescue is not imminent and water is numbing cold, or if worse rapids follow, then strike out for the nearest shore.

5. EXTEND YOUR FEET DOWNSTREAM when swimming rapids to fend against rocks. LOOK AHEAD. Avoid possible entrapment situations; rock wedges, fissures, strainers, brush, logs, weirs, reversals, and souse holes. Watch for eddies and slack water so that you can be ready to use these when you approach. Use every opportunity to work your way toward shore.

6. If others spill, GO AFTER THE BOATERS. Rescue boats and equipment only if this can be done safely.

V. INTERNATIONAL SCALE OF RIVER DIFFICULTY

If rapids on a river generally fit into one of the following classifications, but the water temperature is below 50 degrees F., or if the trip is an extended trip in a wilderness area, the river should be considered one class more difficult than normal.

CLASS I.   Moving water with a few riffles and small waves. Few or no obstructions.

CLASS II.   Easy rapids with waves up to 3 feet, and wide, clear channels that are obvious without scouting. Some maneuvering is required.

CLASS III.   Rapids with high, irregular waves often capable of swamping an open canoe. Narrow passages that often require complex maneuvering. May require scouting from shore.

CLASS IV.   Long, difficult rapids with constricted passages that often require precise maneuvering in very turbulent waters. Scouting from shore is often necessary, and conditions make rescue difficult. Generally not possible for open canoes. Boaters in covered canoes and kayaks should be able to Eskimo roll.

CLASS V.   Extremely difficult, long, and very violent rapids with highly congested routes which nearly always must be scouted from shore. Rescue conditions are difficult and there is significant hazard to life in event of a mishap. Ability to Eskimo roll is essential for kayaks and canoes.

CLASS VI.   Difficulties of Class V carried to the extreme of navigability. Nearly impossible and very dangerous. For teams of experts only, after close study and with all precautions taken.

VI. A NEW SYSTEM OF UNIVERSAL RIVER SIGNALS

STOP: Potential hazard ahead. Wait for "all clear" signal before proceeding, or scout ahead. Form a horizontal bar with your paddle or outstretched arms. Move up and down to attract attention, using a pumping motion with paddle or flying motion with arms. Those seeing the signal should pass it back to others in the party.

HELP/EMERGENCY: Assist the signaller as quickly as possible. Give three long blasts on a police whistle while waving a helmet, or lifevest over your head in a circular motion. If a whistle is not available, use the visual signal alone. A whistle is best carried on a lanyard attached to the shoulder of a life vest.

ALL CLEAR: Come ahead. (In the absence of other directions, proceed down the center.) Form a vertical bar with your paddle or one arm held high above your head. Paddle blade should be turned flat for maximum visibility. To signal direction or a preferred course through a rapid around obstruction, lower the previously vertical "all clear" by 45 degrees toward the side of the river with the preferred route. Never point toward the obstacle you wish to avoid.

Signalling system devised by AWA committee composed of Jim Sindelar, Tom McCloud, O.K. Goodwin, Bev Hartline, Walt Blackadar, and Charles Walbridge. Illustrations by Les Fry.

APPENDIX C

Books on Canoeing and Kayaking Techniques

Kayaking. Jay Evans and Robert Anderson.
   The Stephen Green Press, Brattleboro, VT (1975).
Basic River Canoeing. Robert McNair.
   Buck Ridge Ski Club, Swarthmore, PA (1968).
Recreational White Water Canoeing. Thomas Foster.
   Leisure Enterprise, 8 Pleasant St., Millers Falls, MA (1978).
The All Purpose Guide to Paddling. Dean Norman.
   Great Lakes Living Press, Matteson, IL (1976).
Boat Builder's Manual. Charlie Walbridge, ed.
   Wildwater Designs, Penllyn, PA 19422 (1979).
The Complete Wilderness Paddler. J. W. Davidson and J. Rugge.
   Alfred A. Knopf Inc., New York, NY (1976).
Canoeing. The American National Red Cross.
   Doubleday and Co., Garden City, NY (1977).
Running the Rivers of North America. Peter Wood.
   Barre Publishing, Barre, MA (1978).
Canoeing. Mike Michaelson and Keith Ray.
   Henry Regnery Co., Chicago, IL (1975).
Whitewater Rafting. William McGinis.
   Times Books, NY (1975).

White Water Handbook

Pole, Paddle, and Portage. Bill Riviere.
　Little, Brown and Co., Boston, MA (1969).
A Guide to Big Water Canoeing. David Herzog.
　Contemporary Books Inc., Chicago, IL (1978).
Living Canoeing. Alan Byde.
　Adam and Charles Black Ltd., London (1972).
You, Too, Can Canoe. John Foshee
　Stride Publishers Inc., Huntsville, AL (1977).
Building and Repairing Canoes and Kayaks.
　Jack Brosius and David LeRoy.
　Contemporary Books Inc., Chicago, IL (1978).
Wildwater: The Sierra Club Guide to Kayaking and White Water
　Boating. Lito Tejada-Flores. Sierra Club Books,
　San Francisco, CA (1978).
The Canoe and White Water. C.E.S. Franks.
　Univ. of Toronto Press, Toronto (1977).
Wilderness Canoeing. John Malo.
　Collier Press (1971).

Index

ABOUT THE A.M.C.

The Appalachian Mountain Club is a non-profit volunteer organization of over 25,000 members. Centered in the northeastern United States with headquarters in Boston, its membership is worldwide. The A.M.C. was founded in 1876, making it the oldest organization of its kind in America. Its existence has been committed to conserving, developing, and managing dispersed outdoor recreational opportunities for the public in the Northeast and its efforts in the past have endowed it with a significant public trust; its volunteers and staff today maintain that tradition.

Ten regional chapters from Maine to Pennsylvania, some sixty committees, and hundreds of volunteers supported by a dedicated professional staff join in administering the Club's wide-ranging programs. Besides volunteer organized and led expeditions, these include research, backcountry management, trail and shelter construction and maintenance, conservation, and outdoor education. The Club operates a unique system of eight alpine huts in the White Mountains, a base camp and public information center at Pinkham Notch, New Hampshire, a new public service facility in the Catskill Mountains of New York, five full-service camps, four self-service camps, and nine campgrounds, all open to the public. Its Boston headquarters houses not only a public information center but also the largest mountaineering library and research facility in the U. S. The Club also conducts leadership workshops, mountain search and rescue, and a youth opportunity program for disadvantaged urban young people. The A.M.C. publishes guidebooks, maps, and America's oldest mountaineering journal, *Appalachia*.

We invite you to join and share in the benefits of membership. Membership brings a subscription to the monthly bulletin *Appalachia*; discounts on publications and at the huts and camps managed by the Club; notices of trips and programs; and, association with chapters and their meetings and activities. Most important, membership offers the opportunity to support and share in the major public service efforts of the Club.

Membership is open to the general public upon completion of an application form and payment of an initiation fee and annual dues. Information on membership as well as the names and addresses of the secretaries of local chapters may be obtained by writing to: The Appalachian Mountain Club, 5 Joy Street, Boston, Massachusetts 02108, or calling during business hours 617-523-0636.